Popular Complete Smart Series

• Advanced •
Complete
MathSmart

Grade 7

 Proud Sponsor of the Math Team of Canada 2017

ISBN: 978-1-77149-205-8

ISBN: 978-1-77149-205-8

A Message to Parents

Advanced Complete MathSmart is an extension of our bestselling *Complete MathSmart* series. This series focuses on challenging word problems that require the application of the math concepts and skills that children have learned in the *Complete MathSmart* series.

The two sections in this book are designed to gradually develop your child's problem-solving and critical-thinking skills. In Section 1, each unit covers one core topic and begins with basic skills questions, followed by problem-solving questions that increase in difficulty as the unit progresses. It reinforces your child's math concepts and skills in the topic in focus. Working through this section, your child should be able to proficiently explain and illustrate the solutions to the word problems.

Section 2 provides abundant critical-thinking questions, each combining multiple topics from Section 1. The topics are integrated in different ways to provide a wide range of complex and challenging questions that help stimulate your child's mathematical reasoning and develop his or her critical-thinking skills.

An answer key with step-by-step solutions is also provided at the end of this comprehensive book. All the solutions are presented in a clear and organized way to allow your child to have a thorough understanding of the math concepts.

Advanced Complete MathSmart will not only improve your child's core math understanding and skills, but also develop his or her critical-thinking skills which are essential in solving daily life challenges.

Your Partner in Education,
Popular Book Co. (Canada) Ltd.

ISBN: 978-1-77149-205-8

Advanced Complete MathSmart

Section 1:
Basic Problem-solving Questions

ISBN: 978-1-77149-205-8

Contents

Section 2:
Critical-thinking Questions

ISBN: 978-1-77149-205-8

ISBN: 978-1-77149-205-8

Section 1:
Basic Problem-solving Questions

ISBN: 978-1-77149-205-8

Multiples and Factors

solving a variety of word problems that involve finding the GCF and LCM

Math Skills

Complete the factor trees and write each number as a product of factors. Find the GCF and LCM of each set of numbers.

①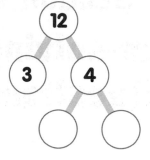

②

12 = _____ × _____ × 3   18 = _____

③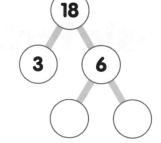

④

24 = _____   28 = _____

⑤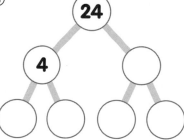

⑥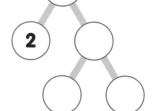

36 = _____   40 = _____

⑦
12
18
GCF: _____
LCM: _____

⑧
12
24
GCF: _____
LCM: _____

⑨
18
24
GCF: _____
LCM: _____

⑩
12
36
GCF: _____
LCM: _____

⑪
12
18
24
GCF: _____
LCM: _____

⑫
12
24
40
GCF: _____
LCM: _____

⑬
18
36
40
GCF: _____
LCM: _____

ISBN: 978-1-77149-205-8

Problem Solving

I'm preparing identical fruit baskets with apples and oranges.

If Daisy has 20 apples and 30 oranges, how many fruit baskets can she prepare at most?

Solution:

Step 1: Use a factor tree to find the product of factors for each number.

20

30

20 = ☐ × ☐ × ☐   30 = ☐ × ☐ × ☐

Step 2: Find the GCF.

GCF of 20 and 30: ☐ × ☐ = ☐

Step 3: Write a concluding sentence.

Daisy can prepare ☐ fruit baskets at most.

① Refer to the question above. How many apples and oranges will there be in each fruit basket?

There will be _____ apples and _____ oranges.

ISBN: 978-1-77149-205-8

② Melissa has 25 balloons and 35 glow sticks that she wants to divide into identical gift bags.

a. What is the greatest number of gift bags that Melissa can make?

Hints

Find the GCF.

Melissa can make _____ gift bags.

b.

How many of each item will go into each gift bag?

Melissa

_____ balloons and _____ glow sticks will go into each gift bag.

③ Michael has bought 32 tulips and 40 lilies to arrange into the greatest number of identical floral centrepieces. How many tulips and lilies will there be in each centrepiece?

There will be _____ tulips and _____ lilies in each centrepiece.

ISBN: 978-1-77149-205-8

④ Mrs. Kerr is going to pack 9 baby carrots, 12 crackers, and 18 grapes into lunch boxes. How many of each food item will there be in a lunch box if she packs the items into the greatest number of identical lunch boxes?

There will be _____ baby carrots, _____ crackers, and _____ grapes in each lunch box.

⑤ At a summer camp, there are 39 boys and 26 girls. They will be divided into groups of boys and groups of girls.

a. The groups have the same number of children with the greatest number of children in each group. How many groups of boys will there be?

There will be _____ groups of boys.

b.

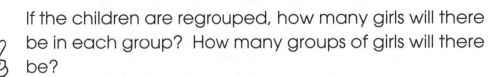
3 boys and 2 girls get sick and will not participate.

If the children are regrouped, how many girls will there be in each group? How many groups of girls will there be?

There will be _____ girls in each group. There will be _____ groups of girls.

⑥ Patties are sold in packages of 8 and buns are sold in packages of 12. Harvey makes each burger with 1 patty and 1 bun.

a. Harvey wants to buy enough patties and buns to make burgers with no patties or buns left over. At least how many burgers will Harvey make?

_____

b. How many packages of patties and buns will Harvey buy?

_____

⑦ The eastbound bus arrives every 6 minutes and the westbound bus arrives every 8 minutes. If both buses arrive now, after how many minutes will both buses arrive at the same time again?

_____

⑧ There is a lamppost every 11 m and a tree every 7 m.

Lana

There is a lamppost and a tree in front of my house. How many metres from my house will there be both a lamppost and a tree?

_____

ISBN: 978-1-77149-205-8

⑨ A printing company made copies of a 30-sheet manual and a 40-sheet novel. The numbers of sheets used for the copies of both books were the same.

a. What was the least number of sheets used for each book?

_____

b. How many copies of each book were there?

_____

⑩ The admission fee for a game fair was $12 for children and $26 for adults. A group of children and adults from a summer camp went to the fair. The total fee for the children and that for the adults were the same.

a. What was the lowest fee the group paid in all?

_____

b. How many children and adults were there in the group if the lowest fee was paid?

_____

⑪ I can evenly divide all my postcards into stacks of 5, 9, or 15.

If there are fewer than 100 postcards, how many postcards could Tom have?

Tom

_____

⑫ Ms. Nguyen is making sandwiches for a potluck. She has 96 pieces of bacon, 72 leaves of lettuce, and 48 slices of tomato. How many identical sandwiches can she make at most? How much of each ingredient will each sandwich have?

_____

⑬ A teacup ride makes 15 rotations and a carousel makes 18 rotations every time they run. If both rides made the same number of rotations, at least how many times did each ride run?

_____

⑭ Jupiter orbits the Sun about every 12 years, Saturn every 30 years, and Uranus every 84 years. If the 3 planets were last in alignment in 1926, when will they align again?

_____

⑮ Train A arrives every 18 minutes and Train B arrives every 27 minutes. If both trains arrived at 6:45 p.m., what was the previous time when the trains arrived together?

_____

   ISBN: 978-1-77149-205-8

⑯ Miriam has 2 bags of beads.

a. If she wants to make identical bracelets using all the beads, how many bracelets can she make at most?

_____

b. How many red beads and blue beads will there be in each bracelet?

_____

c. Miriam wants to order more beads so that she will have the same number of red beads and blue beads. At least how many beads of each colour will she have?

_____

⑰ Mark is making two shelves by stacking up the boxes shown. Each shelf is made up of boxes of the same size.

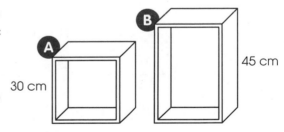

a. If the heights of the two shelves are the same, at least how tall is each shelf?

_____

b. Mark puts boards horizontally into each box so that the height of each section is the same. What is the maximum height of each section?

Perfect Squares and Square Roots

solving a variety of word problems that involve perfect squares and square roots

Math Skills

① Find the area of each square.

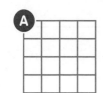

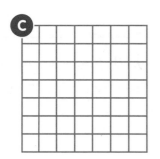

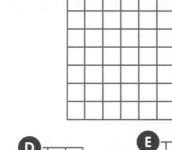

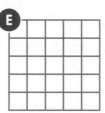

Area of Squares

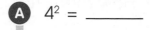

A 4^2 = _____

B 8^2 = _____

C 7^2 = _____

D 3^2 = _____

E 5^2 = _____

② Find the perfect squares. Then find the square roots.

a. **Perfect Squares**

1^2 = _____ 2^2 = _____

3^2 = _____ 4^2 = _____

5^2 = _____ 6^2 = _____

7^2 = _____ 8^2 = _____

9^2 = _____ 10^2 = _____

11^2 = _____ 12^2 = _____

13^2 = _____ 14^2 = _____

15^2 = _____ 16^2 = _____

17^2 = _____ 18^2 = _____

19^2 = _____ 20^2 = _____

b. **Squares Roots**

$\sqrt{1}$ = _____ $\sqrt{4}$ = _____

$\sqrt{9}$ = _____ $\sqrt{16}$ = _____

$\sqrt{25}$ = _____ $\sqrt{36}$ = _____

$\sqrt{49}$ = _____ $\sqrt{64}$ = _____

$\sqrt{81}$ = _____ $\sqrt{100}$ = _____

$\sqrt{121}$ = _____ $\sqrt{144}$ = _____

$\sqrt{169}$ = _____ $\sqrt{196}$ = _____

$\sqrt{225}$ = _____ $\sqrt{256}$ = _____

$\sqrt{289}$ = _____ $\sqrt{324}$ = _____

$\sqrt{361}$ = _____ $\sqrt{400}$ = _____

ISBN: 978-1-77149-205-8

Problem Solving

Try This!

The numbers of apples the boys picked are recorded as shown. Who picked the most apples?

Edwin	Wesley	Joe
150	16^2	$\sqrt{289}$

Solution:

Step 1: Evaluate the square and the square root.

$$16^2 = 16 \times 16 = \boxed{}$$

$$\sqrt{289} = \boxed{}$$

The ones digit of the square root must be 3 or 7.

There is a relationship between the ones digit of a number and the ones digit of its square. Use this relationship to help you determine the square root of a number.

Step 2: Compare the numbers.

$$\boxed{} < \boxed{} < \boxed{}$$

Step 3: Write a concluding sentence.

$\boxed{}$ picked the most apples.

$$8^2 = 64$$
$$18^2 = 324$$
$$28^2 = 784$$

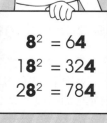

① Olivia has 12 dozen gumdrops. How many gumdrops does she have?

Olivia has _____ gumdrops.

ISBN: 978-1-77149-205-8

② A jigsaw puzzle has 19 rows and 19 columns. How many puzzle pieces are there in the puzzle?

There are _____ puzzle pieces in the puzzle.

③ Logan's bedroom has a square window that has a side length of 36 cm. What is the area of the window?

The area of the window is _____ cm².

④

The square rug has a side length of 2 m. The rectangular rug has an area of 3.5 m². I bought the one with the greater area.

Which rug did Roy buy?

Roy

Roy bought the _____ .

ISBN: 978-1-77149-205-8

⑤ Denise has a piece of dough as shown.

a. What is the area of the dough?

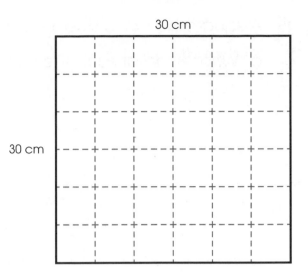

30 cm

30 cm

The area of the dough is _____ cm².

b. Denise cuts the pieces of dough along the dotted line as shown to make cookies. How many cookies will there be?

There will be _____ cookies.

c.

What is the area of each piece of cookie dough?

Denise

The area of each piece of cookie dough is _____ cm².

⑥ A square tile has a side length of 5 cm.

a. What is the area of the square tile?

_____

b. A design is made by tiling 25 rows of square tiles. Each row has 25 tiles. What is the area of the design?

_____

⑦
Canadian checkers is played on a 12 by 12 square board. The tiles alternate between black and white.

a. How many tiles are there in total?

_____

b. The side length of each tile is 2 cm. What is the area of the board?

_____

ISBN: 978-1-77149-205-8

⑧ Murray's square farm has an area of 324 m². What is the side length of his farm?

Hints

$$324 \leftarrow \begin{array}{l} 2 \times 2 = \mathbf{4} \\ 8 \times 8 = 6\mathbf{4} \end{array}$$

So, the ones digit of the square root of 324 must be 2 or 8.

_____

⑨ Michael is arranging 484 chairs for an outdoor concert. If he wants the number of rows and the number of chairs in each row to be the same, how many rows will there be?

_____

⑩ Nana is making the largest square quilt possible by sewing pieces of small square fabrics together. If she has 500 pieces, how many pieces will be left after making the quilt?

_____

⑪ The area of a square painting is 320 cm². Will the painting fit inside a square frame that has a side length of 18 cm?

_____

ISBN: 978-1-77149-205-8

⑫ Conrad has a box of 1000 square tiles. He uses them to tile the greatest possible square. How many tiles will there be in each row of the square?

_____

⑬ Carla bought 2 square mirrors. The areas of the mirrors are 729 cm² and 961 cm². What is the difference between the side lengths of the mirrors?

_____

⑭ The design of a tile is shown.

  a. What is the area of the tile?

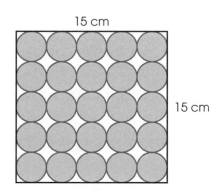

15 cm

15 cm

_____

  b. A square flooring design has an area of 9 m². How many tiles are needed for each row?

_____

  c. How many circles does the flooring design have?

_____

ISBN: 978-1-77149-205-8

⑮ Felix put 9 square photos together to make a collage that has an area of 576 cm².

   a. What is the side length of the collage?

_____

   b. What is the perimeter of each square photo?

_____

⑯ Roberto cut the fringe off of a 121-cm² square cloth and used it to trim one side of a square towel.

   a. What is the perimeter of the towel?

_____

   b. What is the area of the towel?

_____

⑰ Catherine built a prism with blocks. The prism has 25 layers. Each layer has 5 rows of 5 blocks. How many blocks did Catherine use to build the prism?

_____

ISBN: 978-1-77149-205-8

Integers

solving a variety of word problems that involve operations with integers

 Math Skills

① Use the number lines to find the answers.

a.

-2 + 4 = _____

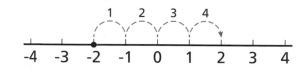

b.

-11 – (-6) = _____

c.

-8 + (-5) = _____

② 3 + (-9) = _____

③ (-10) + (-7) = _____

④ (-5) + 6 = _____

⑤ 17 – (-3) = _____

⑥ 14 – (-14) = _____

⑦ (-4) – (5) = _____

⑧ (-3) × 1 = _____

⑨ 5 × (-7) = _____

⑩ (-6) × (-9) = _____

⑪ 14 ÷ (-7) = _____

⑫ (-27) ÷ 3 = _____

⑬ (-64) ÷ (-8) = _____

⑭ 3 + (-2) × (-1)

= 3 + _____

= _____

⑮ (-3) × 8 + 16

= _____ + 16

= _____

⑯ 18 – (-2) + 8

= _____ + 8

= _____

⑰ 32 ÷ (-8) – 9

=

=

⑱ (-8) × 2 × (-3)

=

=

⑲ (-13) × (-7) + (-9)

=

=

⑳ 64 ÷ (-2) ÷ (-4)

=

=

㉑ 30 ÷ ((-7) + (-8))

=

=

㉒ (-16) ÷ (-4) × (-3)

=

=

ISBN: 978-1-77149-205-8

Problem Solving

Try This!

The temperature was -8°C yesterday and -4°C today. How much warmer was today than yesterday?

Solution:

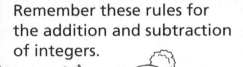
Remember these rules for the addition and subtraction of integers.

Step 1: **Write a number sentence.**

-4 – (-8) = ☐

Step 2: **Use a number line if needed.**

-5 -4 -3 -2 -1 0 1 2 3 4 5

Step 3: **Write a concluding sentence.**

It was ☐ °C warmer today.

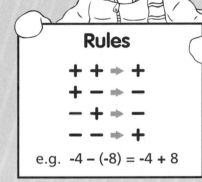

Rules

+ + ➙ +
+ – ➙ –
– + ➙ –
– – ➙ +

e.g. -4 – (-8) = -4 + 8

① The current temperature is -16°C and it is expected to drop by 12°C overnight.

a. What is the expected overnight temperature?

The expected overnight temperature is _____°C.

b. The temperature in the morning was -10°C. What is the difference between the current temperature and the morning temperature?

Tips

To find the difference, subtract the bigger number by the smaller number.

The difference is _____°C.

ISBN: 978-1-77149-205-8

② Nancy and Conrad played a game. Their scores are recorded as shown.

Children's Scores

	Nancy	Conrad
Round 1	-6	8
Round 2	9	-11

a. How many more points did Conrad get than Nancy in Round 1?

Conrad got _____ more points than Nancy in Round 1.

b. How many points in total did each child get?

• Nancy

Nancy got _____ points in total.

• Conrad

Conrad got _____ points in total.

c.

Did I have a higher total score? If so, by how many points?

Conrad

Nancy

_____

_____

ISBN: 978-1-77149-205-8

③ Cynthia's bank account had a balance of -$35.

   a. How much does she have in her account after depositing $27?

   Cynthia has $_____ in her account.

   b. If Cynthia wants to have a balance of $50, how much more does she need to deposit?

   Cynthia needs to deposit $_____ more.

④ A bird is flying at an elevation of 11 m and a fish is swimming at an elevation of -3 m.

   a. What is their difference in elevation?

Tips

> An elevation below the sea level is indicated by a negative number.

   Their difference in elevation is _____ m.

   b. A turtle is swimming at an elevation of -15 m. What is the difference in elevation between the fish and the turtle?

   The difference in elevation is _____ m.

ISBN: 978-1-77149-205-8

⑤   Cuba is -5 hours from Ireland and Egypt is +1 hour from Ireland.

     a. What is the time difference between Cuba and Egypt?

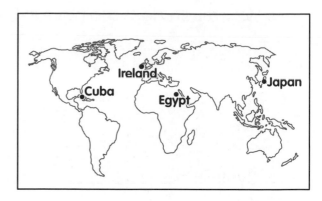

_____

     b. Cuba is -13 hours from Japan. What is the time difference between Japan and Ireland?

_____

⑥   Mr. Li bought 5 shares of a stock. The change for each share was -$4 yesterday.

     a. What was the total change of the shares he bought?

_____

     b. Today, the change for each share is -$8.

> What is the total change of the shares from yesterday and today?

Mr. Li

_____

ISBN: 978-1-77149-205-8

⑦ The average change in profit was expected to be -$25 each day.

    a. What was the expected total change in profit over 5 days?

_____

    b. If the actual change was -$35, what was the average change each day over the 5 days?

_____

⑧ An elevator went 6 floors down and its change in elevation was -18 m. What was the change in elevation for each floor?

_____

⑨

The average change in value of this signed baseball was -$13 over the last 3 years.

What was the total change in value?

Kylie

_____

 ISBN: 978-1-77149-205-8

⑩

Here is your weather forecast for cities in Ontario.

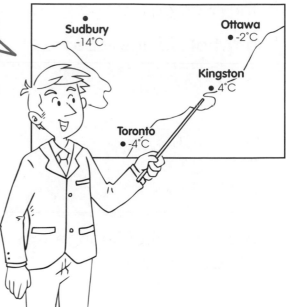

Sudbury
-14°C

Ottawa
● -2°C

Kingston
● 4°C

Toronto
● -4°C

a. What is the difference in temperature between

• Kingston and Ottawa?

_____

• Toronto and Sudbury?   • Ottawa and Sudbury?

_____   _____

b. What is the average temperature of the cities?

_____

c. If in the following week, Toronto has 2 days of -6°C, 1 day of -5°C, and 4 days of -1°C, what will the average temperature of the week be?

_____

ISBN: 978-1-77149-205-8

⑪ Andrew, Zack, and Ryan entered a trivia contest. A contestant gets 3 points for each correct answer and -2 points for each incorrect answer.

a. Find the score of each child.

• Andrew: 3 correct, 5 incorrect

_____

• Zack: 2 correct, 3 incorrect

_____

• Ryan: 4 correct, 2 incorrect

_____

b. Who won the contest? How many more points did the 1st-place contestant get than the 3rd-place contestant?

_____

c.

> How many more questions should I have answered correctly to tie the winner?

Andrew

_____

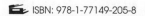

Fractions

solving a variety of word problems that involve fractions with like and unlike denominators

 Math Skills

① $\dfrac{4}{5} + \dfrac{7}{10}$

② $\dfrac{11}{12} - \dfrac{1}{3}$

③ $\dfrac{5}{8} \times \dfrac{4}{15}$

④ $\dfrac{2}{3} \div \dfrac{2}{9}$

⑤ $\dfrac{9}{10} + \dfrac{5}{6} =$ _____

⑥ $1\dfrac{7}{8} + 2\dfrac{1}{6} =$ _____

⑦ $\dfrac{25}{12} + 2\dfrac{5}{6} =$ _____

⑧ $\dfrac{4}{7} + 2\dfrac{19}{21} =$ _____

⑨ $1\dfrac{6}{7} - \dfrac{13}{14} =$ _____

⑩ $\dfrac{20}{9} - 1\dfrac{1}{3} =$ _____

⑪ $2\dfrac{4}{5} - \dfrac{22}{15} =$ _____

⑫ $\dfrac{11}{15} - \dfrac{13}{20} =$ _____

⑬ $\dfrac{3}{10} \times \dfrac{5}{9} =$ _____

⑭ $\dfrac{7}{8} \times 1\dfrac{1}{8} =$ _____

⑮ $\dfrac{4}{5} \times 3\dfrac{1}{3} =$ _____

⑯ $\dfrac{15}{4} \times 2\dfrac{2}{5} =$ _____

⑰ $\dfrac{1}{3} \div \dfrac{7}{12} =$ _____

⑱ $2 \div \dfrac{8}{9} =$ _____

⑲ $3\dfrac{1}{3} \div \dfrac{5}{9} =$ _____

⑳ $7\dfrac{1}{5} \div \dfrac{2}{3} =$ _____

㉑ $2\dfrac{1}{4} \times 2\dfrac{2}{3} - 4\dfrac{1}{5}$

㉒ $1\dfrac{7}{20} \div 1\dfrac{4}{5} + 2\dfrac{5}{8}$

㉓ $\left(\dfrac{14}{5} - 2\dfrac{1}{3}\right) \times 3\dfrac{3}{14}$

㉔ $8\dfrac{1}{2} \div \left(\dfrac{5}{2} + 2\dfrac{3}{5}\right)$

ISBN: 978-1-77149-205-8

Problem Solving

Try This!

> Last week, I played football for $2\frac{1}{4}$ h and basketball for $1\frac{3}{5}$ h.

How much time did Arnold spend on sports last week?

Solution:

Step 1: **Write a number sentence.**

$$2\frac{1}{4} + 1\frac{3}{5} = \boxed{}$$

Step 2: **Add the fractions.**

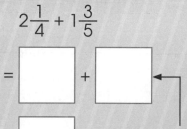

$$2\frac{1}{4} + 1\frac{3}{5}$$

$$= \boxed{} + \boxed{} \longleftarrow$$

$$= \boxed{}$$

Rewrite the fractions with the same denominator.

Step 3: **Write a concluding sentence.**

Arnold spent $\boxed{}$ h on sports last week.

① Lucas used $1\frac{5}{7}$ m of ribbon to tie a gift and $\frac{13}{14}$ m to tie a bow. How many metres of ribbon did he use in all?

Lucas used _____ m of ribbon.

ISBN: 978-1-77149-205-8

② To make his own trail mix, Jordan mixed $2\frac{1}{2}$ cups of almonds, $1\frac{4}{5}$ cups of sunflower seeds, and $\frac{3}{4}$ cup of other ingredients. How many cups of trail mix did Jordan make in total?

Jordan made _____ cups of trail mix.

③ Robin diluted $3\frac{2}{3}$ L of concentrated fertilizer with $4\frac{5}{6}$ L of water.

a. How much fertilizer did Robin make?

It is good practice to write answers in simplest form.

Robin made _____ L of fertilizer.

b. After spraying the fertilizer in his garden, Robin has $2\frac{5}{12}$ L of fertilizer left. How much fertilizer was used?

_____ L of fertilizer was used.

ISBN: 978-1-77149-205-8

④ Nathan ran $4\frac{5}{6}$ km and Violet ran $1\frac{2}{5}$ km more than Nathan.

a. How much did Violet run?

Violet ran _____ km.

b.

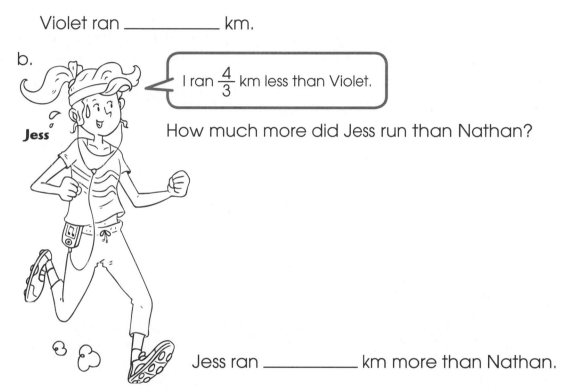

I ran $\frac{4}{3}$ km less than Violet.

How much more did Jess run than Nathan?

Jess ran _____ km more than Nathan.

⑤ Paulina had 10 kg of road salt. She used $4\frac{1}{6}$ kg on her driveway and another $3\frac{4}{9}$ kg on the sidewalk. How much road salt is left?

_____ kg of road salt is left.

ISBN: 978-1-77149-205-8

⑥

> For 1 serving of lasagna, $\frac{1}{6}$ can of tomato sauce is needed.

How many cans of tomato sauce did Mrs. Grand use to make 12 servings?

Mrs. Grand

_____

⑦ A mug fills $\frac{1}{7}$ of a pot. How much of the pot will be filled with $5\frac{1}{4}$ mugs of water?

_____

⑧ One batch of cookies requires $2\frac{1}{3}$ cups of sugar. Eddie wants to make $3\frac{1}{2}$ batches of cookies.

a. How much sugar is needed?

_____

b. Each batch makes 24 cookies. How many cookies will be made?

_____

ISBN: 978-1-77149-205-8

⑨ Each episode in a TV series is $\frac{3}{4}$ h long. The entire series is $18\frac{3}{4}$ h long.

a. How many episodes are there in the series?

_____

b. How long is each episode in minutes?

_____

⑩ A carousel makes $5\frac{5}{9}$ revolutions in a minute.

a. How many revolutions will the carousel make in $3\frac{3}{5}$ minutes?

_____

b. How many minutes will it take to make 15 revolutions?

_____

ISBN: 978-1-77149-205-8

⑪ A box of chocolates is $\frac{1}{4}$ full with 33 pieces. How many pieces of chocolate were there when it was full?

_____

⑫ Jonathan can swim $1\frac{3}{4}$ laps in $2\frac{1}{3}$ min. How many laps can he swim in $\frac{5}{6}$ min?

_____

⑬ Jenna collected 4 L of rainwater but she spilled $1\frac{2}{3}$ L of it. The remaining rainwater now fills $\frac{2}{5}$ of a container. What is the capacity of the container?

_____

⑭ Mr. Smith spent $3\frac{2}{3}$ hours, $2\frac{5}{6}$ hours, and $3\frac{1}{5}$ hours working on his science experiment in the last 3 days.

a. On average, how many hours did Mr. Smith spend working on his experiment each day?

_____

b.

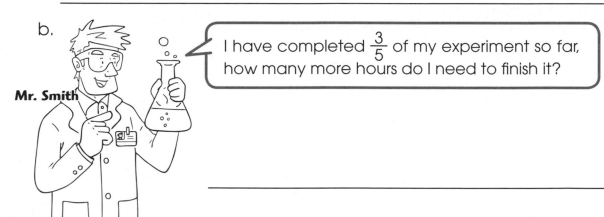

I have completed $\frac{3}{5}$ of my experiment so far, how many more hours do I need to finish it?

Mr. Smith

_____

ISBN: 978-1-77149-205-8

⑮ Tony's plant is $32\frac{1}{8}$ cm tall. If it grows $\frac{5}{6}$ cm every week, how tall will Tony's plant be after 9 weeks?

_____

⑯ Martin drinks $7\frac{1}{2}$ cups of water in $1\frac{1}{3}$ days and Bryan drinks $5\frac{5}{12}$ cups in $\frac{5}{6}$ day.

a. How many more cups of water does Bryan drink in a day?

_____

b. A jug holds 20 cups of water. How many days will it take Martin to finish the jug of water?

_____

⑰ A group of grades 7 and 8 students are on a field trip. $\frac{9}{20}$ of the students are boys and $\frac{7}{15}$ of the students are in grade 7.

a. If there are 33 girls on the field trip, how many students are there in total?

_____

b.
> If there are 15 grade 7 boys, what fraction of the girls are in grade 7?

_____

ISBN: 978-1-77149-205-8

solving a variety of word problems that involve decimals

 Math Skills

①
$$\begin{array}{r} 2\overset{1}{5}.67 \\ +\ 18.45 \\ \hline 34.12 \end{array}$$

②
$$\begin{array}{r} \overset{0\ \overset{9}{9}\ \overset{9}{9}}{10.00} \\ -\ 2.76 \\ \hline 07.24 \end{array}$$

③
$$\begin{array}{r} \overset{2}{7}.7 \\ \times\ 4.3 \\ \hline \overset{1}{23}.1 \\ -30\ 80 \\ \hline 33.11 \end{array}$$

④
$$\begin{array}{r} 05.2 \\ 4\overline{)20.8} \\ -20\downarrow \\ \hline 0\ 8 \end{array}$$

⑤ $14.63 + 2.9 = \underline{17.53}$

⑥ $20.18 + 6.083 = \underline{26.263}$

⑦ $17.03 + 2.17 = \underline{19.20}$

⑧ $3.19 + 31.9 = \underline{35.09}$

⑨ $6.86 + 0.021 = \underline{6.881}$

⑩ $7.35 + 4.017 = \underline{11.367}$

⑪ $4.87 - 2.53 = \underline{2.34}$

⑫ $10.32 - 1.9 = \underline{8.42}$

⑬ $0.7 - 0.07 = \underline{0.77}$

⑭ $2.43 - 0.177 = \underline{2.253}$

⑮ $3.5 - 1.305 = \underline{2.205}$

⑯ $8 - 0.818 = \underline{7.182}$

⑰ $6.82 \times 1.6 = \underline{109.12}$

⑱ $3.4 \times 3.006 = \underline{10.2216}$

⑲ $4.62 \times 2.9 = \underline{11.398}$

⑳ $27.04 \times 4.95 = \underline{23.5970}$

㉑ $2.03 \times 9.12 = \underline{18.5136}$

㉒ $6.026 \times 1.7 = \underline{\hspace{2cm}}$

㉓ $12.69 \div 1.5 = \underline{8.46}$

㉔ $0.075 \div 0.5 = \underline{\hspace{2cm}}$

㉕ $1.98 \div 0.03 = \underline{0.66}$

㉖ $4.068 \div 0.18 = \underline{\hspace{2cm}}$

㉗ $49.44 \div 2.4 = \underline{20.6}$

㉘ $0.0602 \div 0.02 = \underline{\hspace{2cm}}$

㉙ $(0.75 + 0.79) \div 1.1$

㉚ $1.65 \times (18.779 - 16.297)$

㉛ $3.56 \times 2.45 + 1.6 \div 0.2$

㉜ $(2.43 + 1.45) \times (4.836 - 2.336)$

ISBN: 978-1-77149-205-8

Problem Solving

Alastor added 5.5 mL of lemon juice to his 250.83-mL tea to make lemon tea. How much lemon tea did he make?

Solution:

| Step 1: | **Write a number sentence.** |

250.83 + 5.5 = ☐

> To add or subtract decimals, their decimal points must be aligned. Once the decimals are aligned, the rest of the digits will be aligned correctly.

| Step 2: | **Do the addition.** |

```
  2 5 0.8 3
+     5.5 0   ← Add "0" as a place holder.
  ┌─────────┐
  │         │
  └─────────┘
```
⌐ The decimal points for the addends and the sum must all be aligned.

| Step 3: | **Write a concluding sentence.** |

Alastor made ☐ mL of lemon tea.

---

① Refer to the question above. Alastor added 14.608 mL of syrup to his lemon tea.

a. How much lemon tea is there now?

There is _____ mL of lemon tea.

b. If Alastor drinks 130.43 mL of it, how much lemon tea will be left?

_____ mL of lemon tea will be left.

ISBN: 978-1-77149-205-8

②
A pair of basketball shoes costs $34.99 and a basketball costs $19.95.

a. How much do the items cost in all?

The items cost $_____ in all.

b. $7.14 in tax is added to the shoes and basketball. What is the total cost?

The total cost is $_____ .

③ Nathan had $150 and paid $97.62 for a new skateboard. How much money does Nathan have left?

Nathan has $_____ left.

ISBN: 978-1-77149-205-8

④ Gordon's route to work is 9.07 km long and a shortcut is 1.238 km shorter. How long is the shortcut?

The shortcut is _____ km long.

⑤ Jocelyn weighs 2 grapes on a scale. They weigh 16.273 g.

   a. If Jocelyn removes the smaller grape, the weight will become 9.109 g. How much does the smaller grape weigh?

The smaller grape weighs _____ g.

b.

The total weight of these 3 grapes is 25 g.

What is the weight of the third grape?

The weight of the third grape is _____ g.

⑥ Kylie wants US $20. The exchange rate for US $1 was 1.26 yesterday and 1.305 today. How much in Canadian dollars would she need if she did the exchange

a. yesterday?

_____

b. today?

_____

⑦

The scale of this map is 1 cm to 200 m.

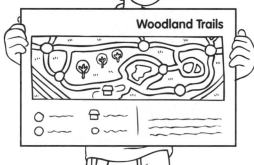

Woodland Trails

a. Two ponds are 4.219 cm apart on the map. What is the actual distance?

_____

b. Trail A is 2.301 cm longer than Trail B on the map. How much longer is Trail A actually?

_____

ISBN: 978-1-77149-205-8

⑧
> My data plan charges $0.025 for each megabyte. The cost of streaming this video will be $2.12.

How many megabytes are used to stream the video?

Meredith

_____

⑨ A litre of gas cost $1.025. Lina spent $45.51 on gas. How many litres of gas did she fill?

_____

⑩ Cassidy paid $44.16 for 345 kWh of electricity last month.

a. On average, how much did 1 kWh of electricity cost?

_____

b. The price of each kWh of electricity depends on the time of the day. $35.07 was spent on non on-peak hours. If the price for each on-peak hour was $0.18/h, how many on-peak hours were charged?

Tips

As of 2016, there are 3 rates on the price of each kWh of electricity, the on-peak rate, mid-peak rate, and off-peak rate.

_____

ISBN: 978-1-77149-205-8

⑪ Nelson mixes 2.6 L of soda, 4.825 L of orange juice, and 0.855 L of lime juice to make a jar of fruit punch.

a. How much fruit punch will there be if he makes 2 jars?

_____

b. Each jar of fruit punch is poured equally into 16 cups. How many millilitres of fruit punch is there in 1 cup?

_____

⑫ Marsha has saved $21.35 and she expects that her savings will be 2.4 times her current savings by the end of the year.

a. How much will there be in her savings?

_____

b. Marsha will use $22.39 of her savings on a shirt and 0.55 of the remaining on a gift. How much will the gift be?

_____

⑬ Conner gained 2.408 kg, which is 0.05 of his mass now. How much did he weigh before gaining weight?

_____

ISBN: 978-1-77149-205-8

⑭ The sale prices of the items are shown on the flyer.

    a. How much do 3 T-shirts and 2 pairs of jeans cost?

    Liza's Clothing Sale

    $15.99

    $32.65

    $26.65

_____

    b. How much more do 2 sweaters cost than 1 T-shirt and 1 pair of jeans?

_____

    c. For the price of 5 T-shirts, how many sweaters can be bought?

_____

⑮ Janice spent $20.57 in total renting a leaf blower. The cost of the rental included a $8.79 cleaning fee plus $14.725 for every litre of gasoline used. How many litres of gasoline did Janice use?

_____

⑯ Beef costs $15.25/kg and pork costs $17.45/kg. How much more does 1.202 kg of pork cost than 0.824 kg of beef?

_____

ISBN: 978-1-77149-205-8

Percents

solving a variety of word problems that involve percents

 Math Skills

① **Percent ➡ Fraction**

a. 20% $= \dfrac{20}{100} =$ _____

b. 32% = _____ = _____

c. 10% = _____ = _____

d. 6% = _____ = _____

e. 84% = _____ = _____

f. 105% = _____ = _____

② 15% of 200

$= 200 \times 15\%$

$= 200 \times \dfrac{}{100}$

= _____

③ 25% of 64

④ 50% of 2

⑤ 1% of 300

⑥ 8% of 50

⑦ 120% of 95

⑧ **Percent ➡ Decimal**

a. 27% = _____

b. 43% = _____

c. 5% = _____

d. 18% = _____

e. 112% = _____

f. 3% = _____

g. 94% = _____

⑨ 10% of 90

$= 90 \times 10\%$

$= 90 \times$ _____

= _____

⑩ 75% of 44

⑪ 6% of 150

⑫ 50% of 12

⑬ 48% of 200

⑭ 105% of 10

ISBN: 978-1-77149-205-8

Problem Solving

Try This!

A book that cost $25 is now on sale for 20% off. What is the sale price?

Solution:

Step 1: **Find the discounted amount.**

Think 20% of $25 is the discounted amount.

Discounted amount: $25 × 20%

$$= \$25 \times \boxed{}$$

$$= \$\boxed{}$$

Step 2: **Find the sale price.**

Think Subtract the original price by the discounted amount to get the sale price.

Sale price: $25 – $ $\boxed{}$

$$= \$\boxed{}$$

Step 3: **Write a concluding sentence.**

The sale price of the book is $ $\boxed{}$.

① Shauna wants to buy a bike that costs $190.50. If the bike is currently sold at 15% off, how much does Shauna need to pay?

Tips

Round the answers of money values to 2 decimal places.

Shauna needs to pay $_____ .

ISBN: 978-1-77149-205-8

②
> The table shows the sales tax rates of some provinces in Canada as of 2016.

Province	Tax Rate
Alberta	5%
Ontario	13%
British Columbia	12%

For a jacket that costs $125, how much does it cost after tax in

a. Alberta?

It costs $_____ in Alberta.

b. Ontario?

c. British Columbia?

It costs $_____ in Ontario.   It costs $_____ in British Columbia.

③ Rebecca wants to make a $180 purchase online during a 15% off promotion period. What will the total cost be after a 14% tax is applied?

> Tax is applied on all discounted prices.

The total cost will be $_____ .

ISBN: 978-1-77149-205-8

④ Mr. Apple has 260 apple trees on his farm. 80% of them grow red apples, 15% of them grow green apples, and the rest grow yellow apples. How many trees grow yellow apples?

_____ trees grow yellow apples.

⑤ There are 56 children in a summer camp. 25% of them are boys. How many girls are there?

There are _____ girls.

⑥ Of the 180 Internet users surveyed, 35% of them last surfed the Internet with phones, 20% with tablets, and the rest with computers. How many of the users last surfed the Internet with computers?

_____ users last surfed the Internet with computers.

⑦ Mrs. Blink mixed some bleach with water to make a 1050-mL cleaning solution. 5% of the solution is bleach. How much water was added?

_____ mL of water was added.

ISBN: 978-1-77149-205-8

⑧ Laura used 30% of a roll of 5-m ribbon to make a bow. How much ribbon remains?

_____

⑨ A can had 3.85 L of paint. Michael spilled 8% of it. How much paint is still in the can?

_____

⑩ A dress shirt is marked down from $61 to $45.75.

a. What is the discount in percent?

_____

b. A $27.50 belt also has the same discount in percent. How much is the belt after the discount?

_____

 ISBN: 978-1-77149-205-8

⑪ On a bookshelf, there are 204 novels, 51 comic books, and 45 magazines. What percent of the books are

a. novels?

_____

b. not magazines?

_____

⑫ Gene used 45.2 g from a stick of butter and there is 67.8 g remaining. What percent of the stick of butter remains?

_____

⑬

I bought a $17.95 calculator and a $15.55 stapler and paid $38.19 after taxes.

What was the tax rate?

_____

⑭ Vivian surveyed 40 people about the plants in their backyards. 12 of them have flowers only, 14 have trees only, 2 have both, and the rest have none. What percent of the people have

a. flowers only?

_____

b. trees?

_____

⑮ A rectangular wall measures 3 m by 5 m. Olivia painted a triangle that has an area of 3 m² on the wall. What percent of the wall

a. is painted?

_____

b. is not painted?

_____

⑯ Margaret put $1980 into a savings account with a simple annual interest rate of 4%. How much will she have in total after 6 years?

Hints

Simple annual interest is the money amount earned yearly. It is found by multiplying the amount invested by the interest rate.

_____

ISBN: 978-1-77149-205-8

⑰ Ada made a pitcher of lemonade and poured it into a cup. The 250-mL cup of lemonade has 10 mL of syrup.

a. What percent of the lemonade is syrup?

_____

b. If there was 1 L of lemonade in the pitcher, how much syrup was there in the pitcher?

_____

⑱ Joshua has a total of 35 nickels and dimes. 40% of the coins are nickels.

a. How many nickels are there?

_____

b. What percent of the money amount is nickels?

_____

⑲ I harvested 450 tomatoes. 82% of the tomatoes still remain.

How many tomatoes still remain?

Megan

_____

ISBN: 978-1-77149-205-8

7 Ratios and Rates

solving a variety of word problems that involve ratios and rates

Math Skills

① Write the ratios.

a.

★ ★ ★ ★ ★ ★
★ ★ ♥ ♥ ♥ ♥

- ★ : ♥ = ____ : ____
- ♥ : ★ = ____ : ____
- ♥ : all = ____ : ____

b. **A A A A B B B**
   C C 1 1 1 2 3

- **A : C** = ____ : ____
- **B : 2** = ____ : ____
- **C** : all numbers = ____ : ____
- **3** : all letters = ____ : ____

② Write the equivalent ratios.

3:5

9:____

____:25

6:8

3:____

____:24

2:1

4:____

____:8

2:3

____:9

8:____

5:6

10:____

____:30

10:4

____:2

25:____

③ Find the rates.

a.
$10.20

$_____ /muffin

b.
1.5 L

_____ L/box

c.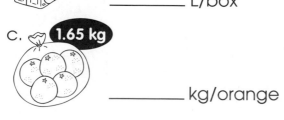
1.65 kg

_____ kg/orange

d. The size of 8 files is 256 MB.

_____ MB/file

e. Ada's heart beats 468 times in 6 min.

_____ beats/min

f. A train travels 198 km in 2.4 h.

_____ km/h

g. There is 34 cm of snow in 0.5 h.

_____ cm/h

ISBN: 978-1-77149-205-8

Problem Solving

The ratios of red candies to blue candies that Vera and Joe have are both 2:3. Vera has 10 red candies. Joe has 12 blue candies. How many candies do they have in all?

Solution:

Step 1: Find the number of blue candies that Vera has.

red to blue = 2:3 = 10:☐

⌐×5⌐
└×5⌐

Step 2: Find the number of red candies that Joe has.

red to blue = 2:3 = ☐:12

⌐×4⌐
└×4⌐

Step 3: Find the total.

10 + ☐ + ☐ + 12 = ☐

Step 4: Write a concluding sentence.

They have ☐ candies in all.

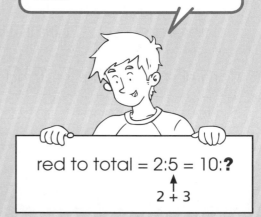

Alternatively, to find the total number of candies Vera has, you can write the ratio of "red to total" first.

red to total = 2:5 = 10:**?**
↑
2 + 3

① Refer to the question above. How many red candies does Vera have if she has

a. 9 blue candies?

b. a total of 30 candies?

Vera has _____ red candies.

Vera has _____ red candies.

ISBN: 978-1-77149-205-8

② The ratio of boys to girls in a class is 3:2.

a. If there are 18 girls in the class, how many more boys than girls are there?

There are _____ more boys in the class.

b. If there are 30 students in all, how many girls are there in the class?

There are _____ girls in the class.

③ Flora has planted roses and tulips in a ratio of 3:4 in her garden.

a. How many more tulips are there if 15 roses have been planted?

There are _____ more tulips.

b.

I have planted 18 roses.

Flora

How many more tulips does she have to plant if 20 of them have been planted?

Flora has to plant _____ more tulips.

ISBN: 978-1-77149-205-8

④ Mr. Howard is mixing paint. The ratio of red paint to blue paint is 2:3 to mix purple paint.

   a. How much purple paint will Mr. Howard get if he uses 6 L of blue paint?

      Mr. Howard will get _____ L of purple paint.

   b. If Mr. Howard wants 15 L of purple paint, how much red paint and blue paint does he need?

      Mr. Howard needs _____ L of red paint and _____ L of blue paint.

⑤ Julia is making salad dressing using vinegar and syrup. The ratio of vinegar to syrup is 5:3. She wants to make 48 mL of dressing.

   a. How much vinegar does she need?

      Julia needs _____ mL of vinegar.

   b. If Julia wants to reduce her sugar consumption and the ratio of vinegar to syrup is now 5:1. How much vinegar does she need instead?

      Julia needs _____ mL of vinegar instead.

⑥ Rhonda can type up to 352 words in 8 minutes.

a. What is Rhonda's typing speed in words/min?

_____

b. How many words can Rhonda type in half an hour?

**Hints**

Remember to make sure all values are in the same unit before calculating.

_____

⑦ Apples are sold at 3 for $1.50 at ValueMart and 5 for $2.35 at FruitShop. Which is the better buy?

_____

⑧ Rosie has the option of buying paper towels in packages of 6 or 20. How much will Rosie save on each roll of paper towels by buying a package of 20?

_____

ISBN: 978-1-77149-205-8

⑨ A plane can complete a 756-km journey in 5 hours. How far can it travel in 8.5 hours?

_____

⑩ Lowell's car can drive 162 km on 15 L of gas. How far can he drive with 75 L?

_____

⑪ Last month, the cost of 12 muffins was $6.84. If the cost for each muffin increased by 7¢ this month, how much do 10 muffins cost now?

_____

⑫ A bike can cover 3 km in 0.25 h and it travelled for 1.5 h. The speed of a car is 50 km/h. How long will it take the car to cover the same distance as the bike?

_____

ISBN: 978-1-77149-205-8

⑬ The mass of red beads to green beads is in the ratio of 5:6. The total mass of the beads is 220 g. The cost is $2 for 80 g of beads.

a. What is the mass of the red beads?

_____

b. What is the rate in $/g? What is the cost of buying the beads?

_____

c. If $7.70 was spent on the beads, how many grams of red beads were bought?

_____

⑭ It costs $128.85 to rent a car for 3 days and $96.55/day for a van.

a. If Maria rents for 5 days, how much more will it cost to rent a van?

_____

b.

> My budget on car rental is $600. Am I able to rent a van? If not, how much more do I need?

Maria

_____

ISBN: 978-1-77149-205-8

⑮ Michelle is making her own Neapolitan ice cream. She wants a ratio of 2:1 for vanilla to chocolate ice cream, and a ratio of 5:3 for vanilla to strawberry ice cream.

　a. For 500 g of chocolate ice cream, how much strawberry ice cream is needed?

Hints

Find the ratio of all 3 flavours.

_____

　b. What is the weight of each flavour in 1.68 kg of Neapolitan ice cream?

_____

⑯ The ratio of the amount of time Peter spends on reading to playing sports is 2:3. Peter spent 135 min on playing sports last week.

　a. How many hours did he spend on reading?

_____

　b. Peter read 33 pages last week. What was his rate in pages/h?

_____

⑰ Sammy and Davis work at a shop. Sammy earned $9/hour. After Sammy received a raise, the ratio of Sammy's pay to Davis's pay changed from 3:4 to 4:3. How much will Sammy earn if he works 40 hours?

_____

ISBN: 978-1-77149-205-8

solving a variety of word problems that involve finding the perimeter and area of shapes and finding the surface area and volume of prisms

 Math Skills

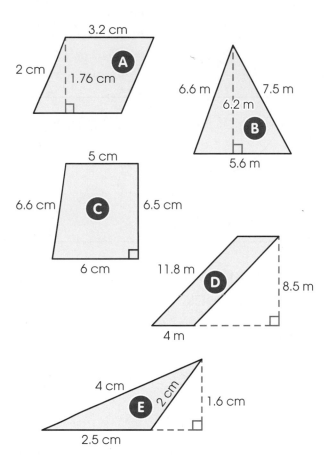

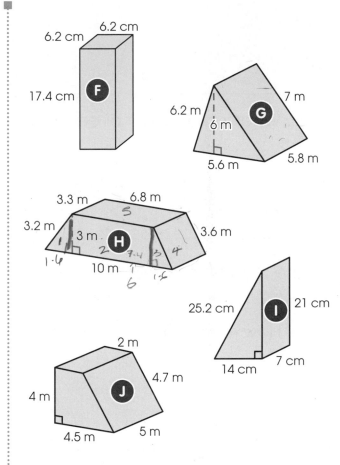

Shape	Perimeter	Area
A	10.4	5.632 cm²
B	19.7	34.72 cm²
C	23.11	39 cm²
D	15.8	34 cm²
E	8.5	4 cm²

Shape	Surface Area	Volume
F	107.88	1276.112 cm³
G	147.28	148.4 cm³
H	458.96	~166.32
I		
J		

ISBN: 978-1-77149-205-8

 **Problem Solving**

Try This!

Marie has a stamp that is in the shape of a trapezoid as shown. What is its area?

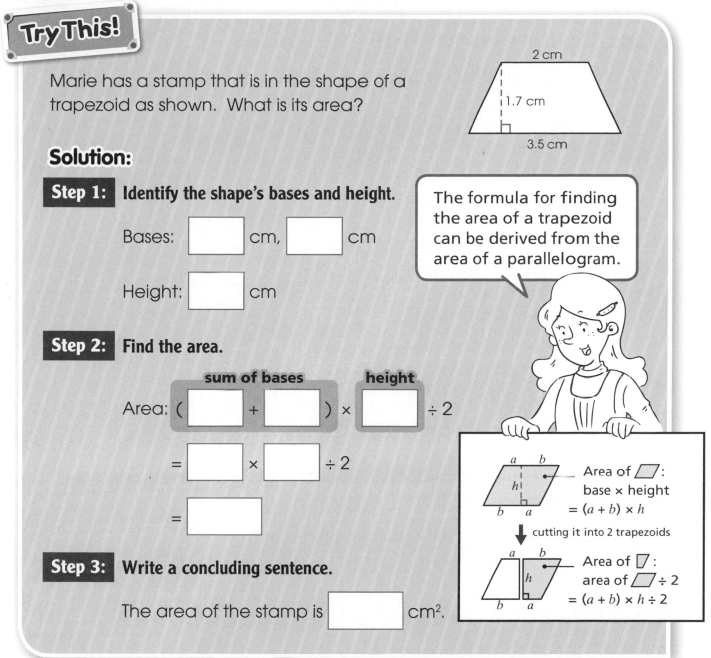

2 cm

1.7 cm

3.5 cm

Solution:

Step 1: Identify the shape's bases and height.

Bases: ☐ cm, ☐ cm

Height: ☐ cm

> The formula for finding the area of a trapezoid can be derived from the area of a parallelogram.

Step 2: Find the area.

Area: (☐ + ☐) × ☐ ÷ 2
(sum of bases)   (height)

= ☐ × ☐ ÷ 2

= ☐

Area of ▱:
base × height
= (a + b) × h

↓ cutting it into 2 trapezoids

Area of ▱:
area of ▱ ÷ 2
= (a + b) × h ÷ 2

Step 3: Write a concluding sentence.

The area of the stamp is ☐ cm².

① Wilson's boat has a triangular sail that has a base of 3.8 m and a height of 7.1 m. What is the area of the sail?

The area of the sail is _____ m.

ISBN: 978-1-77149-205-8

② Mr. Henkings has a rectangular backyard that has the dimensions as shown. He added a walkway which divides the backyard into a triangular patio and a garden that is in the shape of a trapezoid.

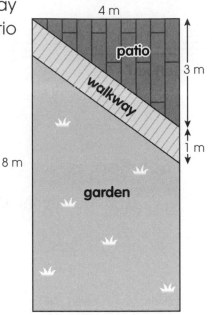

a. What is the area of the patio?

   The area of the patio is _____ m².

b. What is the area of the garden?

   The area of the garden is _____ m².

③ The trapezoid is composed of an equilateral triangle and a parallelogram that has an area of 85.5 cm².

a. What is the height of the parallelogram?

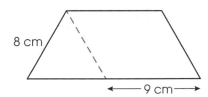

   The height of the parallelogram is _____ cm.

b. What is the area of the trapezoid?

   The area of the trapezoid is _____ cm².

ISBN: 978-1-77149-205-8

④

I sewed 2 identical rhombus-shaped fabric pieces together. Each fabric piece had a perimeter of 1.8 m.

a. What is the perimeter of the sewn fabric piece?

The perimeter is _____ m.

b. The height of the sewn fabric piece is 0.5 m. What is the area of the new fabric piece?

Hints

A rhombus is a special kind of parallelogram that has 4 equal sides.

The area of the new fabric piece is _____ m².

⑤ The dimensions of a kite are as shown. The area of the shaded triangle is 96 cm².

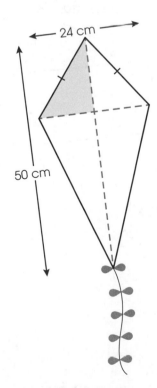

← 24 cm →

50 cm

a. What is the height of the shaded triangle?

The height of the shaded triangle is _____ cm.

b. What is the area of the kite?

The area of the kite is _____ cm².

ISBN: 978-1-77149-205-8

⑥ A jack-in-the-box is a cube that has a side length of 15 cm and it is made out of cardboard.

a. What is the volume of the jack-in-the-box when it is closed?

_____

b. How much cardboard is needed?

_____

⑦ A gift box is a triangular prism as shown.

a. What is the volume of the gift box?

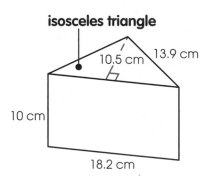

isosceles triangle

10.5 cm

13.9 cm

10 cm

18.2 cm

_____

b. How much wrapping paper is needed for the gift box?

_____

ISBN: 978-1-77149-205-8

⑧ Jackson glued 2 prisms together to make a rectangular prism as shown.

   a. What is the volume of Prism A?

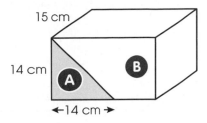

   _____

   b. The volume of Prism B is twice the volume of Prism A. What is the surface area of the rectangular prism?

   _____

⑨ Rosita wants to build a skateboard ramp with the dimensions shown. The area of the trapezoid is 3 m².

   a. What is the height of the ramp?

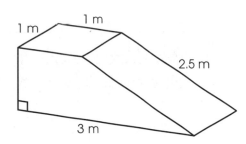

   _____

   b. Rosita wants to paint the entire ramp except the bottom. How much area will be painted?

   _____

ISBN: 978-1-77149-205-8

⑩ Theo stacked 2 blocks as shown to make a triangular prism.

a. What is the volume of the top block?

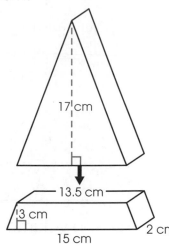

_____

b. What is the volume of the stacked triangular prism?

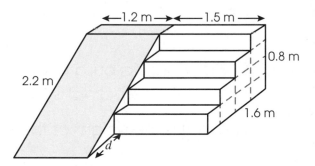

_____

⑪ There is a skateboard ramp next to a staircase. The dimensions of the steps are uniform.

a. What is the volume of the staircase?

_____

b. The staircase and the ramp have the same volume. d represents the difference in length. What is d?

_____

c. The top surfaces of the ramp was painted. How much area was painted?

_____

ISBN: 978-1-77149-205-8

⑫ Simon cuts a cube into 4 smaller square-based prisms. He glues them together to form a design as shown.

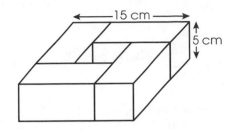

a. What was the volume of the original cube?

_____

b. What is the surface area of the design?

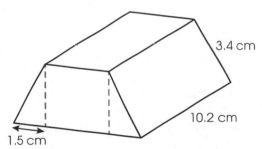

Hints

Remember to include the faces on the inside of the design.

_____

c. How much water can the centre of the design hold?

_____

⑬ Carmen has a block of cheese. She cuts out 2 identical triangular prisms from it along the dotted lines so that only a square-based prism remains. The cut-outs have a total volume of 45.9 cm³.

a. What is the side length of the base of the square-based prism?

_____

b. What is the surface area of the original block of cheese?

_____

ISBN: 978-1-77149-205-8

Angles

solving a variety of word problems that involve angles and triangles

 Math Skills

Complementary Angles

$a + b = 90°$

Supplementary Angles

$a + b = 180°$

Opposite Angles

$a = b$

Corresponding Angles

$a = b$

Alternate Angles

$a = b$

Consecutive Interior Angles

$a + b = 180°$

Angles in a Triangle

$a + b + c = 180°$

①

x = _____   y = _____

②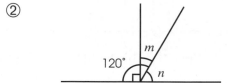

m = _____   n = _____

③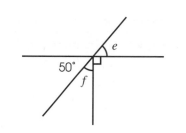

e = _____   f = _____

④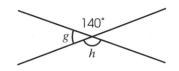

g = _____   h = _____

⑤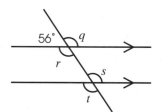

q = _____   r = _____

s = _____   t = _____

⑥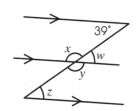

w = _____   x = _____

y = _____   z = _____

⑦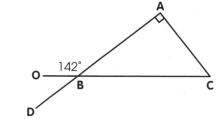

∠ABC = _____

∠ACB = _____

∠OBD = _____

⑧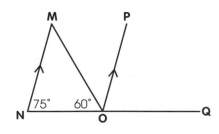

∠NMO = _____

∠NOP = _____

∠POQ = _____

ISBN: 978-1-77149-205-8

 **Problem Solving**

 **Try This!**

Main Street and First Avenue intersect at a 50° angle. What are the sizes of the other 3 angles at the intersection?

Solution:

Step 1: **Draw a diagram.**

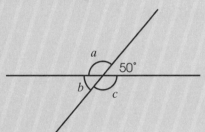

Supplementary angles have a sum of 180°. Opposite angles are equal.

Step 2: **Find the angles.**

By supplementary angles:

$a = 180° - $ ⬚

$= $ ⬚

By opposite angles:

$b = $ ⬚

$c = a = $ ⬚

Step 3: **Write a concluding sentence.**

The sizes of the angles are ⬚ , ⬚ , and ⬚ .

① Jenny drew a triangle with a 37° angle and a 53° angle. Is it a right triangle?

It _____ a right triangle.
is / is not

② In a baseball diamond, Edwin hit a ball at a 29° angle.

a. What is *a*?

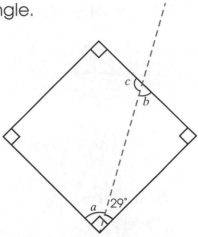

a is _____ .

b. What is *b*?   c. What is *c*?

b is _____ .   *c* is _____ .

③ A flagpole is tethered to the ground by a cable.

a. What is *x*?

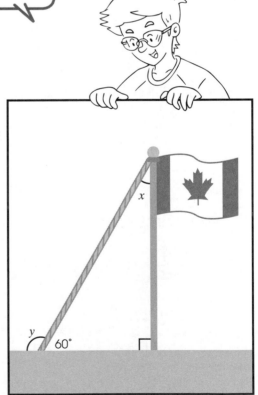

x is _____ .

b. What is *y*?

y is _____ .

                    ISBN: 978-1-77149-205-8

④ A roundabout has 5 exits.

a. What is ∠CRD?

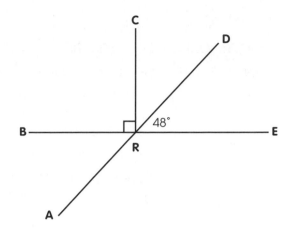

∠CRD is _____ .

b. What is ∠ARE?

∠ARE is _____ .

c. What is the size of the angle that Exit A and Exit C make?

The size of the angle is _____ .

d.

Exit F will be added to the roundabout. It bisects ∠ARE.

Draw to show Exit F. What is ∠ARF?

Tips

"Bisect" means "to divide into 2 equal halves."

∠ARF is _____ .

ISBN: 978-1-77149-205-8

⑤ Ms. Allen is doing a science experiment on light reflection. She finds that the angle at which the laser beam hits the mirror is the same as the beam's reflection.

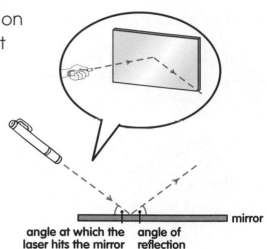

angle at which the laser hits the mirror angle of reflection

mirror

a. If Ms. Allen points the beam at the mirror at 37°, what is the angle between the beam and its reflection?

_____

b. If the angle between the beam and its reflection is 128°, what is the angle of reflection?

_____

⑥ Vason bent a piece of wire into a "W".

a. What is i?

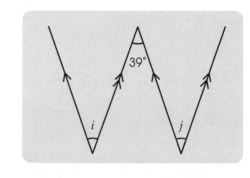

_____

b. What is j?

_____

c. If the segments are all equal in length, is the "W" symmetrical? How do you know?

_____

_____

ISBN: 978-1-77149-205-8

⑦ Three power lines intersect as shown. Without a protractor,

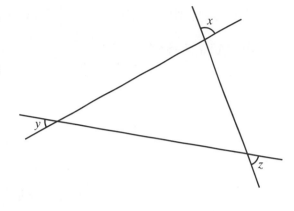

a. can you find the values of x, y, and z? Explain.

_____

_____

b. can you find the sum of Angles x, y, and z? Explain.

_____

_____

_____

⑧ A symmetrical window drape covers part of a rectangular window.

a. What is a?

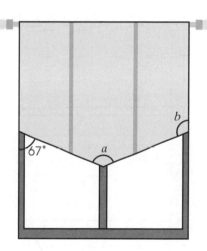

_____

b. What is b?

_____

ISBN: 978-1-77149-205-8

⑨ Look at the shed with 2 identical doors as shown.

a. What is x?

_____

b. 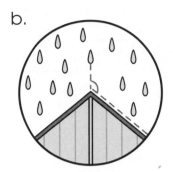 If raindrops fall straight down onto the roof, at what angle will they slide down the roof?

_____

⑩ Randall designed his own bookshelf. The blueprint is shown below.

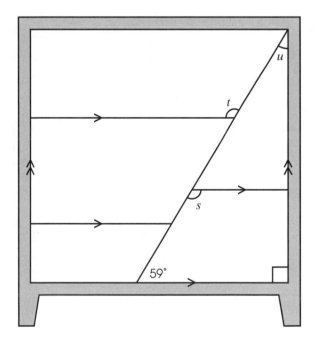

a. What is s?

_____

b. What is t?

_____

c. What is u?

d. Is there another way to find u? If so, show your work.

_____ _____

ISBN: 978-1-77149-205-8

⑪ Look at the map shown.

6th Ave., 7th Ave., and 8th Ave. are parallel to one another.

a. What is *g*?

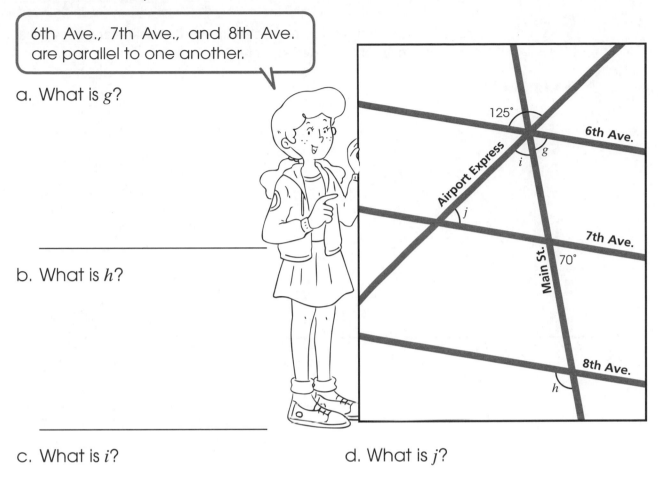

_____

b. What is *h*?

_____

c. What is *i*?

d. What is *j*?

_____   _____

e. A subway line which bisects *i* will be built. Draw to show the subway line on the map.

f. A train track will be built between 7th Ave. and 8th Ave., bisecting Main St. perpendicularly. Draw to show the train track on the map.

g. At what angle will the train track and 8th Ave. intersect?

_____

ISBN: 978-1-77149-205-8

Cartesian Coordinate Plane

solving a variety of word problems that involve coordinates and transformations in all quadrants of the Cartesian coordinate plane

 Math Skills

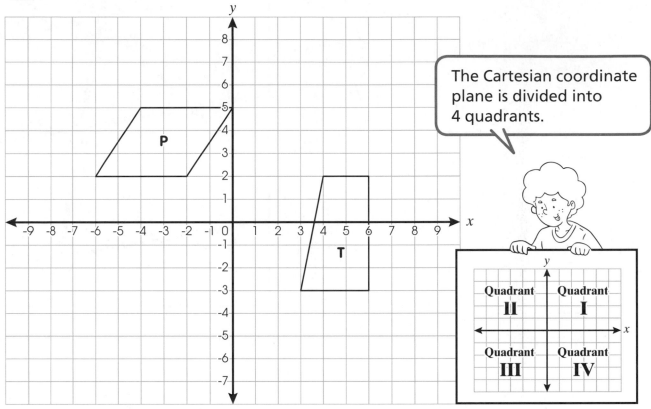

The Cartesian coordinate plane is divided into 4 quadrants.

① Write the coordinates of the vertices of the quadrilaterals.

Parallelogram P

_____

Trapezoid T

_____

② Plot the points. Then connect them to form triangles.

Triangle A	Triangle B	Triangle C
(1,0)	(-4,-2)	(-4,-5)
(1,-5)	(-7,-4)	(0,-5)
(3,-5)	(-2,-4)	(-4,-7)

③ What are the coordinates of the vertices that lie on the

a. *x*-axis? _____

b. *y*-axis? _____

④ Which shape lies in

a. Quadrant III?

_____

b. Quadrant II?

_____

c. both Quadrants I and IV?

_____

ISBN: 978-1-77149-205-8

Problem Solving

Try This!

Harold plots the points below on a Cartesian coordinate plane.

(1,1) (-3,-1) (-2,2) (2,3) (3,-3) (-3,3) (-2,-2) (-1,-1)

How many points are there in each quadrant?

Solution:

Step 1: **Identify the quadrant each point lies in.**

The coordinates of a point tells you in which quadrant the point lies. For example, a point where both coordinates are positive must lie in Quadrant I.

- Quadrant I (+,+):
  (1,1) (2,3)

- Quadrant II (−,+):
  (-2,2) ☐

- Quadrant III (−,−):
  (-3,-1) ☐ ☐

- Quadrant IV (+,−):
  (3,-3)

Step 2: **Write a concluding sentence.**

There are ☐ , ☐ , ☐ , and ☐ points in

Quadrants I, II, III, and IV respectively.

① A triangle with its vertices at (2,1), (3,2), and (1,4) is reflected in the *x*-axis. What are the coordinates of its image?

 Hints

Figure out how the signs of the coordinates will be changed.

The coordinates of its image are _____ , _____ , and _____ .

② Three children drew shapes on the grid.

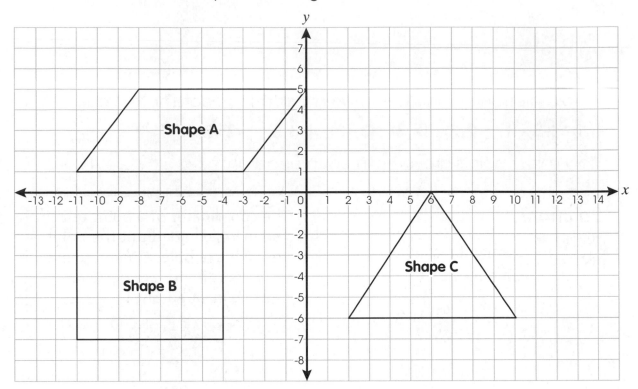

a. Identify the shape each child drew.

• Larry	• Henry	• Diana
_____	_____	_____

b. Whose shape contained the vertices with the

   • greatest x-coordinate?   • smallest y-coordinate?

   _____   _____

c. Jolene also drew a shape that is identical to a $\frac{1}{2}$ rotation about (0,0) of Larry's shape. Draw the shape and write the coordinates of the vertices.

_____

   ISBN: 978-1-77149-205-8

③ Roger was designing a new logo on the Cartesian coordinate plane. He drew a shape with the given coordinates as its vertices.

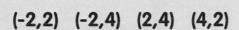

(-2,2) (-2,4) (2,4) (4,2)

a. What is the shape?

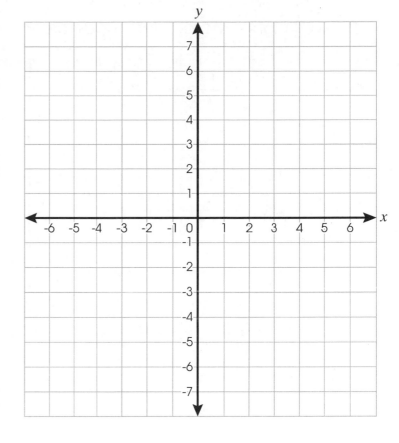

_____

b. Roger performed 3 rotations to complete the design. Find the coordinates of the vertices of the rotated images.

- a $\frac{1}{4}$ clockwise rotation about (0,0)

_____

- a $\frac{1}{2}$ rotation about (0,0)

_____

- a $\frac{1}{4}$ counterclockwise rotation about (0,0)

_____

c.    What is my design's order of rotational symmetry?

Roger

_____

④ Two knights, Marco and Lucas, are trying to save Princess Pear.

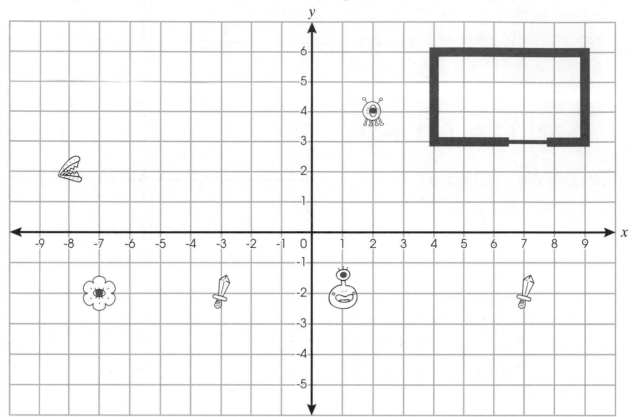

a. Plot to locate each person on the map.

  • Marco: (-7,4)
  • Lucas: (5,-4)
  • Princess Pear: (5,4)

b. Write the coordinates of the monsters below.

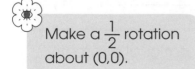 _____    _____

 _____   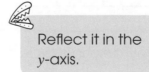 _____

c. Marco and Lucas each picked up the closest sword. Describe their routes.

  • Marco ➔  : _____

  • Lucas ➔  : _____

d. The monsters moved to guard the gate of Princess Pear's cell. Perform the transformations below and draw to show where they were.

Make a $\frac{1}{2}$ rotation about (0,0).

Reflect it in the y-axis.

Translate it 4 units up and 5 units to the right.

e. The knights defeated the monsters and saved Princess Pear. Describe their route to escape from where Princess Pear is to the exit at (-9,-4).

_____

ISBN: 978-1-77149-205-8

⑤ Complete the map and answer the questions.

bridge   subway   bus stop

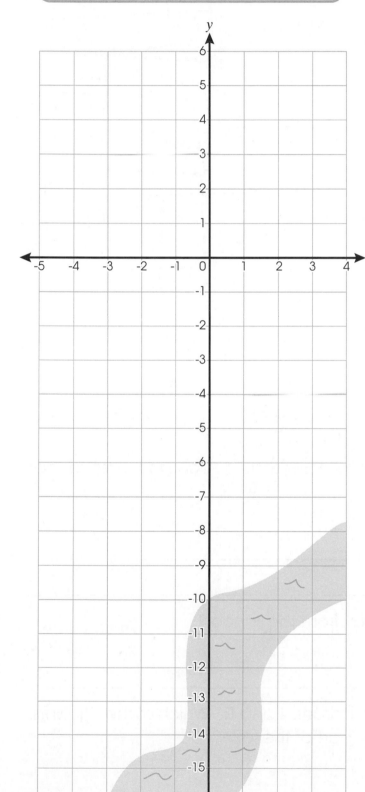

a. Draw to locate the things below.

- bridge

  The two posts on one end of the bridge are at (3,-12) and (3,-14). The other two posts are the reflection in the y-axis.

- subway

  A subway line starts at (-5,5) and runs 7 units to the right, 7 units down, 4 units to the left, 3 units down, and 3 units to the left.

- bus stop

  Bus Stops A, B, and C are at (0,3), (-4,0), and (-4,-9) respectively.

b. Jonas is at the coordinates with the greatest x-coordinate and the smallest y-coordinate possible on the grid. Where is Jonas?

_____

c. How should Jonas travel to get to Bus Stop C if he uses the bridge?

_____

d. A train broke down at the intersection of the subway line and the x-axis. Where did the train break down?

_____

ISBN: 978-1-77149-205-8

⑥ Alice took pictures of a map. Use the pictures to complete the map.

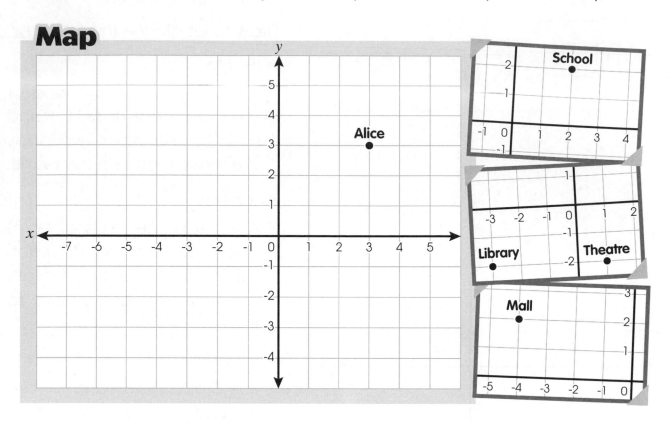

Map

a. Plot the houses of Alice's friends on the map.

Judy
(-1,1)

Keith
(2,4)

Ernice
(-5,3)

George
(-6,-3)

b. Which friend lives closest to Alice? How should Alice go to get to that friend's house?

_____

_____

c. Whose house is the farthest away from the school?

_____

d. There is a lake that lies across Quadrants I and II. Which of these points, (2,-1), (2,3), and (-4,1), could be part of the lake?

_____

ISBN: 978-1-77149-205-8

e.

> The gym is at the reflection of my house in the *x*-axis.
> The café is at the reflection of my house in the *y*-axis.

Alice

Locate the gym and the café on the map. What are their coordinates?

_____

f. The area in Quadrant III is the Town of Sunnyville.   Who lives in the Town of Sunnyville?

_____

g. The quadrant that contains the mall is the Town of Nightvale. Who lives in the Town of Nightvale?

_____

h. Streets on the map run along the grid lines. What is on the same street as

• Ernice's house?   • Keith's house?

_____   _____

• the mall?   • the theatre?

_____   _____

i. Bernard has recently moved. He now lives on the same street as Alice and Judy. What are the possible coordinates of Bernard's house?

_____

j. There is a park that lies on the same streets as Keith's and George's houses. In which quadrant could the park be located?

_____

ISBN: 978-1-77149-205-8

Algebra

solving a variety of word problems that involve evaluating expressions and solving equations

 Math Skills

Evaluate the expressions.

$a = 4$ $b = 2$ $d = 2$

① $2a - 3$

$= 2 \times \underline{\hspace{1.5cm}} - 3$

$= \underline{\hspace{1.5cm}}$

② $10 + 6b$

$= 10 + 6 \times \underline{\hspace{1.5cm}}$

$= \underline{\hspace{1.5cm}}$

③ $26 \div d - 9$

$= 26 \div \underline{\hspace{1.5cm}} - 9$

$= \underline{\hspace{1.5cm}}$

$v = 3$ $w = -1$ $x = 0.5$ $y = \frac{1}{4}$ $z = -2$

④ $18 - 2v \quad = \underline{\hspace{1.5cm}}$ 　　⑤ $9 \div v + 6 \quad = \underline{\hspace{1.5cm}}$

⑥ $1 + wz \quad = \underline{\hspace{1.5cm}}$ 　　⑦ $vw + 4 \quad = \underline{\hspace{1.5cm}}$

⑧ $4v - 2w \quad = \underline{\hspace{1.5cm}}$ 　　⑨ $(11 - v)y \quad = \underline{\hspace{1.5cm}}$

⑩ $x(v + w) \quad = \underline{\hspace{1.5cm}}$ 　　⑪ $2v - 16y \quad = \underline{\hspace{1.5cm}}$

⑫ $wz - 12y \quad = \underline{\hspace{1.5cm}}$ 　　⑬ $(v + x)(v - x) = \underline{\hspace{1.5cm}}$

⑭ $5z \div 4y \quad = \underline{\hspace{1.5cm}}$ 　　⑮ $3(x + 2y) \quad = \underline{\hspace{1.5cm}}$

⑯ $9w + 3v \quad = \underline{\hspace{1.5cm}}$ 　　⑰ $v^2 - wxy \quad = \underline{\hspace{1.5cm}}$

Solve the equations.

⑱ $3n + 2 = 8$ 　　⑲ $a \div 2 + 4 = 9$ 　　⑳ $2(x + 3) = 10$

㉑ $(b - 5) \div 2 = 1$ 　　㉒ $\frac{z}{3} - 4 = -1$ 　　㉓ $6y + y + 5y = 24$

㉔ $16m - 7 = 2m$ 　　㉕ $2b + 9 = b - 6$ 　　㉖ $3(d - 3) = 4d + 2$

ISBN: 978-1-77149-205-8

Problem Solving

The total weight of a box of 12 cookies is 163 g. Janet ate all the cookies and found that the box weighs 7 g. What is the weight of each cookie?

Solution:

Step 1:	Set up an equation.

Think The sum of the weights of the 12 cookies and the box is the total weight.

Let c be the weight of a cookie.

$$12c + 7 = 163$$

↑   ↑   ↑

weight of   weight   total weight
12 cookies   of box

Step 2:	Solve the equation.

$$12c + 7 = 163$$

$$12c + 7 - 7 = 163 - \boxed{}$$ ← Isolate $12c$ by subtracting 7 from both sides.

$$12c = 156$$

$$12c \div 12 = 156 \div \boxed{}$$ ← Isolate c by dividing both sides by 12.

$$c = \boxed{}$$

Step 3:	Write a concluding sentence.

The weight of each cookie is $\boxed{}$ g.

① Allison paid $16 for 2 sandwiches and her change was $4. How much did each sandwich cost?

Each sandwich cost $_____ .

ISBN: 978-1-77149-205-8

② Cory earns $207 in a week at his part-time job. He works 3 shifts a week and each shift is 6 hours long.

a. How much does Cory earn each hour?

Cory earns $_____ each hour.

b. Adding $6 to Melissa's earnings is the same as the double of Cory's earnings for each hour. How much does Melissa earn each hour?

Melissa earns $_____ each hour.

③
I hiked a total of 2 km. In the afternoon, I hiked $\frac{2}{3}$ the distance that I hiked in the morning.

Gabriel

What distance did Gabriel hike in the morning?

Gabriel hiked _____ km in the morning.

ISBN: 978-1-77149-205-8

④ For a charity drive, Ryan collected and sold empty aluminum cans. He collected 8 kg of recycling materials and half of those were from aluminum cans. How many cans did he collect if each can weighs 16 g?

Ryan collected _____ aluminum cans.

⑤ Selma has 2 water bottles. The larger water bottle holds 3 times as much as the smaller one. Together they can hold up to 2 L of water. What capacity does each bottle have?

The larger bottle has a capacity of _____ L and the smaller bottle has

a capacity of _____ L.

⑥
> I'm adding $\frac{3}{4}$ of a can of broth to 284 mL of water to make 500 mL of soup.

How much broth is there in a can?

There is _____ mL of broth in a can.

ISBN: 978-1-77149-205-8

⑦ Brock rented a bike. It costs $8 for the first hour and $4.50 for every half an hour after that. If Brock paid $21.50 for his rental, for how long did he rent the bike?

_____

⑧ A bucket is placed in the backyard to catch water from a dripping faucet. Each minute, the faucet drips 33 mL of water but the bucket leaks 5 mL of water. How long will it take for the bucket to have 140 mL of water?

_____

⑨ Mr. Lohan's age is 4 years less than 3 times Simon's age. The sum of their ages is 44 years.

a. How old is Simon?

_____

b.

In how many years will Mr. Lohan's age be twice my age?

Mr. Lohan

Simon

_____

ISBN: 978-1-77149-205-8

⑩ At a bakery, 5 slices of cake cost $15.30 more than 2 slices of cake.

   a. What is the cost of 1 slice of cake?

_____

   b. During a promotion, Linda bought 6 slices of cake for the cost of 5 slices. How much did she pay for each slice of cake?

_____

⑪ Kate ate $\frac{1}{4}$ of a jar of cookies and Janice ate 3 fewer cookies than Kate. If there are 15 cookies left, how many cookies were there in the jar?

_____

⑫

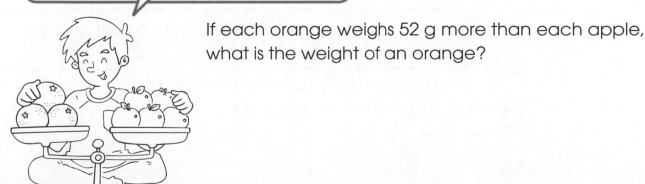

3 oranges weigh as much as 5 apples.

If each orange weighs 52 g more than each apple, what is the weight of an orange?

_____

ISBN: 978-1-77149-205-8

⑬ A hat costs $8 more than a scarf. The total cost of 3 hats and 2 scarves is $69.

a. How much does each item cost?

_____

b. How much do 2 hats and 3 scarves cost?

_____

⑭ Mia's cellphone plan is $16.55 plus 35¢ for each text message. Sia's plan is $26 with unlimited text messages.

a. If their bills this month are equal, how many text messages did Mia send?

_____

b. Last month, their cellphone bills came to a total of $59. How many text messages did Mia send?

_____

⑮

Buying 6 pens in a pack costs $12.54. Buying each pen individually costs $2.30.

How much is saved on each pen by buying a pack instead of 6 individual pens?

_____

ISBN: 978-1-77149-205-8

⑯ Tracy has jogged 110 m and continues to jog at a speed of 3 m/s. Jordan has jogged 30 m and continues to jog at 8 m/s.

a. After how many seconds will they have jogged the same distance?

_____

b. How long will it take Jordan to double Tracy's distance?

_____

⑰ It takes a printer 2 more seconds to print a page in colour than in black and white.

a. If it operated for 54 s and printed 8 pages in black and white and 6 pages in colour, how many seconds did it take to print a page in colour?

_____

b. Samuel printed 2 copies of a book, 1 copy in black and white and the other in colour. If it took the printer 160 s to print the copies, how many pages did the book have?

_____

⑱ Jerry has 24 quarters and dimes with a total of $3.45. How many of each kind of coin is there?

_____

Data Management

solving a variety of word problems that involve measures of central tendency, histograms, circle graphs, and double line graphs

Math Skills

① Find the mean, median, and mode of each set of data.

a.

Ages of Tourists on a Trip
58   35   43
24   40
32   43   20
29   16

mean: _____

median: _____

mode: _____

b.

Heights of Students (cm)
181.5   126.8   141.7
151.2   140.9   126.3
139.4   137.4   122.9

mean: _____

median: _____

mode: _____

c.

Weights of Luggage (kg)
20.82   6.04
19.45   8.33
15.81   5.37
8.33   19.45

mean: _____

median: _____

mode: _____

② Read what the people say. Check ✔ the better graph to represent their data sets. Explain your choice.

a. Mr. Wynn said, "I recorded the heights of 2 plants over the last week. I want to compare their heights."

◯ double line graph

◯ histogram

Reason: _____

_____

b. Adrian said, "I recorded the amount of time spent on each activity in a day. I want to see how much of a day I spent on each activity."

◯ histogram

◯ circle graph

Reason: _____

_____

c. Ms. Leah said, "I want to show the number of people in a mall each hour for the past 10 hours."

◯ circle graph

◯ histogram

Reason: _____

_____

ISBN: 978-1-77149-205-8

Problem Solving

Favourite Colours

Nicole surveyed 300 people about their favourite colour and created this circle graph. What percent of people surveyed chose green as their favourite colour?

Solution:

Step 1: Find the percent of the people who chose green.

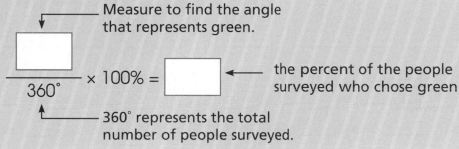

— Measure to find the angle that represents green.

$$\frac{\boxed{}}{360°} \times 100\% = \boxed{}$$ ← the percent of the people surveyed who chose green

360° represents the total number of people surveyed.

Step 2: Find the number of people who chose green.

$$300 \times \boxed{} = \boxed{}$$

Step 3: Write a concluding sentence.

$\boxed{}$ people chose green as their favourite colour.

① Refer to the circle graph above.

a. How many people chose blue as their favourite colour?

b. How many more people chose blue than purple?

_____ people chose blue.

_____ more people chose blue than purple.

ISBN: 978-1-77149-205-8

② An ice cream shop sold a total of 360 scoops of ice cream yesterday. The circle graph shows the number of scoops sold in different flavours.

Scoops Sold in Different Ice Cream Flavours

a. How many scoops were

• chocolate flavoured?

_____

• caramel flavoured?

• mango flavoured?

_____   _____

b. Which 2 flavours took up exactly half of the total number of ice cream scoops sold?

_____

c. Which flavour was more popular than the chocolate flavour? How many more scoops were sold?

_____

d.

Yesterday's daily special was 3 scoops of ice cream in a cone. Each had 1 scoop of strawberry, 1 scoop of chocolate, and 1 scoop of vanilla.

How many daily specials were sold at most?

_____

ISBN: 978-1-77149-205-8

③ Jill surveyed 120 students at her school about their lunch preferences.

a. Complete the table and the circle graph.

Students' Lunch Preferences

Food Item	No. of Votes	Size of Angle
Pizza	48	$360° \times \dfrac{48}{120} = 144°$
Burger	30	
Sandwich	24	
Salad	12	
Others	6	

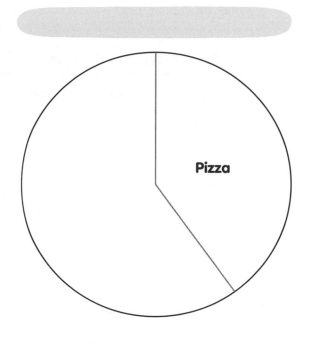

b. Read the circle graph. What food item got

• about 50% of all votes?

• exactly 25% of all votes?

_____

_____

• twice as many votes as "Salad"?

• half as many votes as "Salad"?

_____

_____

c. Do you think that the circle graph is appropriate for representing this data set? Explain.

_____

_____

ISBN: 978-1-77149-205-8

④ Rita booked a flight for one of the days between July 7 and July 13. The fare prices of 2 airlines, GoldAir and FlyWest, are shown in the table. Show the prices in the graph.

Fare Prices of 2 Airlines

Date	GoldAir	FlyWest
July 7	$310	$260
July 8	$300	$275
July 9	$305	$275
July 10	$295	$290
July 11	$300	$290
July 12	$285	$300
July 13	$270	$305

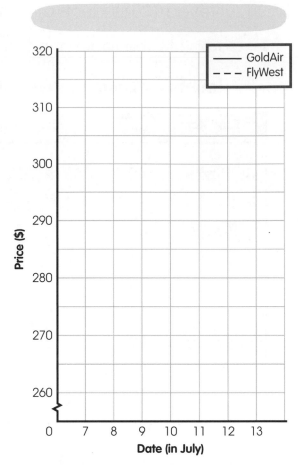

a. What are the mean, median, and mode prices of

• GoldAir?   • FlyWest?

_____   _____

b. Describe the trend in the fare prices for each airline.

• GoldAir : _____

_____

• FlyWest : _____

_____

c. Rita booked a flight with the cheapest fare. Which airline did she book with? For which day was the flight booked?

_____

ISBN: 978-1-77149-205-8

⑤ Mr. Patel owns a dollar store. He shows the store's revenue from January to June using the two graphs below.

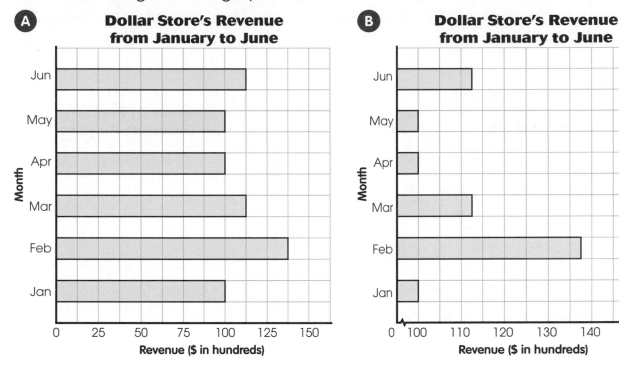

a. Which measure of central tendency do you think best describes this set of data? Explain.

_____

_____

b. If Mr. Patel wanted to show that his store's revenue was steady in the past six months, which graph should he use?

_____

_____

c. If Mr. Patel wanted to show that February had the strongest sales, which graph should he use?

_____

_____

d. Which graph do you think better describes this set of data? Explain your reasoning.

_____

_____

ISBN: 978-1-77149-205-8

⑥ Mr. Denton's class did a science experiment in which the students planted their own seeds. The heights of the plants are measured after a month and are recorded below. Complete the stem-and-leaf plot and the histogram. Then answer the questions.

Record

28 cm	29 cm	4 cm	10 cm
	19 cm	40 cm	8 cm
42 cm	9 cm	24 cm	21 cm
	38 cm	32 cm	3 cm
32 cm	36 cm	13 cm	6 cm
	21 cm	13 cm	16 cm
12 cm	13 cm	21 cm	35 cm

Heights of Plants (cm)

Stem	Leaf
0	
1	
2	
3	
4	

key: 1 | 2 = 12 cm

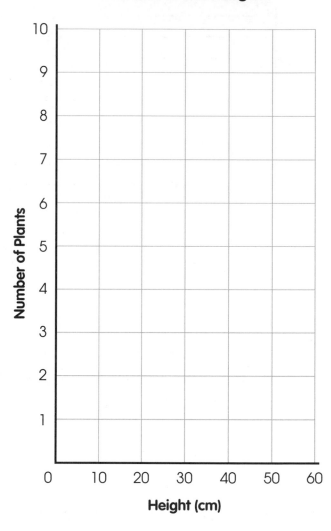

Number of Plants with Different Heights

a. How many students were there in the class?

_____

b. What was the height of

• the tallest plant? •the shortest plant?

_____   _____

ISBN: 978-1-77149-205-8

c. Which range of heights had

    • the most plants?

    • the fewest plants?

_____

_____

d. How many plants were

    • in the 10 cm to 29 cm range?

> **Hints**
>
> In the histogram, add the bars within the given range to find the number of values within that range.

_____

    • shorter than 40 cm?

_____

    • taller than 19 cm?

_____

e. What is the mean height of the plants?

_____

f. In which range does the median height belong?

> **Tips**
>
> Use the stem-and-leaf plot. The values should already be arranged in order.

_____

g. My plant's height is in the most frequent range. Which range is it in?

Ben

_____

ISBN: 978-1-77149-205-8

Probability

solving a variety of word problems that involve probability

 Math Skills

① **Pick a Card!**

a. P(4) = ⬚/⬚ = _____%   b. P(Q) = ⬚/⬚ = _____%

c. P(◆) = _____ = _____   d. P(not 4) = _____ = _____

e. P(♠) = _____ = _____   f. P(letter) = _____ = _____

g. P(J) = _____ = _____   h. P(number) = _____ = _____

i. P(4 or 8) = _____ = _____   j. P(♥ or ◆) = _____ = _____

k. P(not ◆) = _____ = _____   l. P(not a letter) = _____ = _____

② **Spin the Wheels!**

a. P(A) = ⬚/⬚ = _____%

b. P(D) = _____ = _____

c. P(1) = _____ = _____

d. P(2) = _____ = _____

e. P(A or B) = _____ = _____

f. P(1 or 2) = _____ = _____

g. P(not A) = _____ = _____

h.   P(A and 1)
   = P(A) × P(1)

   = _____ × _____

   = _____

   = _____ %

i.   P(B and 2)
   = P(B) × P(2)

   = _____ × _____

   = _____

   = _____ %

ISBN: 978-1-77149-205-8

 **Problem Solving**

Yvonne is playing a game in which she flips a coin and then rolls a dice. What is the probability that she flips a head and rolls a 3?

Solution:

Step 1: **Find the probability of each event.**

P(heads) = ☐

P(3) = ☐

> Independent events are 2 or more events that have no effect on the probability of the other(s). Flipping a head on a coin and rolling a 3 on a dice are independent events.

Step 2: **Multiply the probabilities.**

P(heads and 3)
= P(heads) × P(3)

= ☐ × ☐

= ☐

Step 3: **Write a concluding sentence.**

The probability is ☐ .

To find the probability of independent events A and B occurring, multiply the probabilities of both events.

P(A and B) = P(A) × P(B)

① Refer to the question above. What is the probability that Yvonne flips a tail and rolls an even number?

The probability is _____ .

ISBN: 978-1-77149-205-8

② Raymond picks a card and draws a ball. Find the probabilities in 2 ways.

card

A B C D

ball

A B C D

Way 1 : using multiplication

a. P(A and D)

b. P(B and C)

c. P(C and C)

Way 2 : using a tree diagram

d. P(A and D) = _____

e. P(B and C) = _____

f. P(C and C) = _____

g.  Compare the probabilities. Are they the same? If so, which way do you prefer?

Raymond

_____

_____

_____

ISBN: 978-1-77149-205-8

③ Michael spins both wheels.

a. What is the probability that Michael will get

• two "**1**"?

_____

• a sum of 5?

_____

• two even numbers?

_____

b. If Michael spins the wheel 60 times, about how many times will he get

• two "**1**"?

• a sum of 5?

_____   _____

c. About how many times did I spin the wheels if I got...

Michael

• two "**1**" ten times?

_____

• a sum of 5 ten times?

_____

ISBN: 978-1-77149-205-8

④ Alex is rolling a dice that is labelled 1 to 6 twice.

a. Find the probabilities.

- P(rolling two "3")

- P(rolling 2 numbers less than 5)

_____

- P(rolling 2 even numbers)

- P(rolling 2 of the same number)

_____

b.

I'll multiply the 2 outcomes to get a product.

Complete the table and find the probabilities.

Alex

- P(getting 36 as a product)

✖	1	2	3	4	5	6
1						
2						
3						
4						
5						
6						

_____

- P(getting a perfect square as a product)

_____

c. Can you find the probability of getting 36 as a product without using the table? If so, show your work.

_____

ISBN: 978-1-77149-205-8

⑤ At a restaurant, a machine dispenses 2 different kinds of drinks: lemonade and ginger ale. Each drink comes in 3 sizes: small, medium, and large. What is the probability that the next drink

a. will be a large ginger ale?

_____

b. will be a small lemonade?

_____

c. will not be a small lemonade?

_____

d. The restaurant also sells ice cream. What is the probability that the next order will be a vanilla ice cream in a waffle cone with sprinkles?

Ice Cream Shop

Flavours
• vanilla
• chocolate
• strawberry

Cones
• sugar
• waffle

Toppings
• sprinkles
• chocolate sauce

_____

e. If 60 ice cream cones were sold, about how many of them were not vanilla ice cream in waffle cones with sprinkles?

_____

ISBN: 978-1-77149-205-8

⑥ Linda has 20 white marbles and 20 black marbles. She puts 5 white marbles and 15 black marbles into a box and the remaining marbles into a bag. She picks a marble from the box and a marble from the bag.

a. What is the probability that she will get

Hints

Make a simple diagram to illustrate the scenario.

• 2 black marbles?

_____

• a white marble from the box and a black marble from the bag?

_____

• a black marble from the box and a white marble from the bag?

_____

• a white marble and a black marble?

Hints

The white marble can be from the box or the bag; the same reasoning applies for the black marble.

_____

b. If Linda does 40 trials, about how many times will she get a white marble and a black marble?

_____

ISBN: 978-1-77149-205-8

⑦ These 5 cards are labelled A, B, C, D, and E. I will pick 1 card at random, put it back, and pick another card.

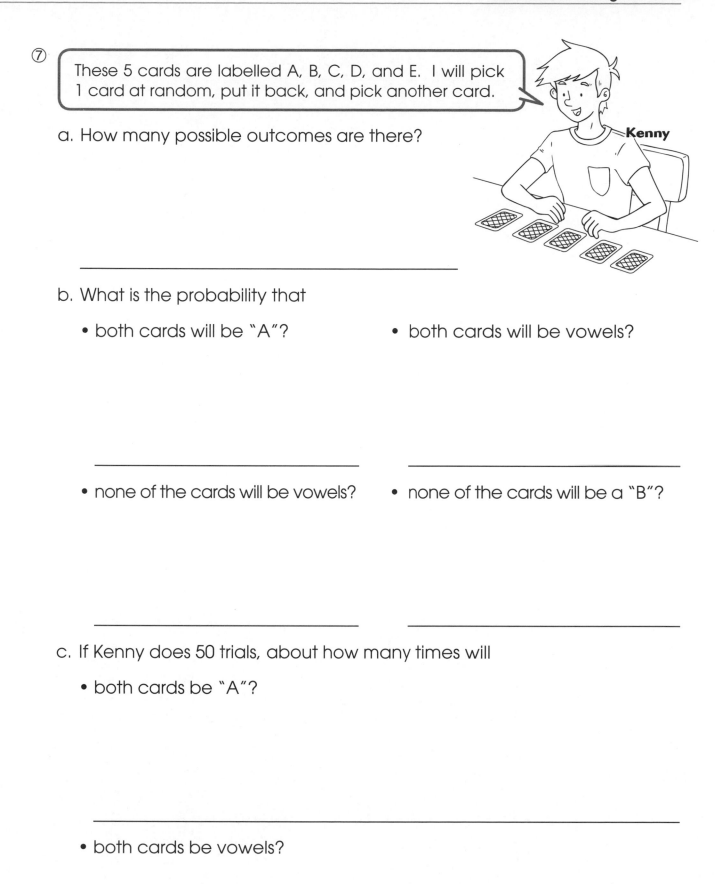

Kenny

a. How many possible outcomes are there?

_____

b. What is the probability that

• both cards will be "A"?

• both cards will be vowels?

_____

• none of the cards will be vowels?

• none of the cards will be a "B"?

_____

c. If Kenny does 50 trials, about how many times will

• both cards be "A"?

_____

• both cards be vowels?

_____

ISBN: 978-1-77149-205-8

ISBN: 978-1-77149-205-8

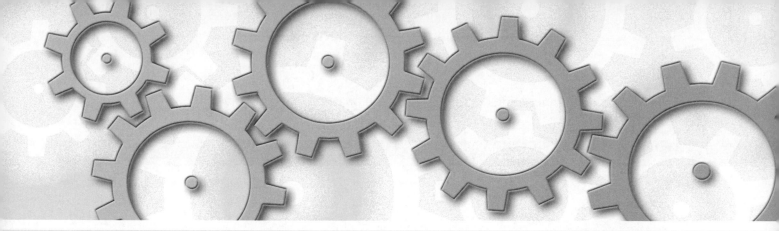

Section 2:
Critical-thinking Questions

ISBN: 978-1-77149-205-8

Students are required to solve multi-step questions which involve various topics in each.

Topics Covered

	Number Sense and Numeration	Measurement	Geometry and Spatial Sense	Patterning and Algebra	Data Management and Probability	My Record ✔ correct ✘ incorrect
1	square roots	measurement				☐
2	fractions decimals			algebra		☐
3	ratios		angles			☐
4	multiples square roots	measurement				☐
5	integers				probability	☐
6	decimals	measurement				☐
7	percents ratios	measurement				☐
8	perfect squares				probability	☐
9	fractions			algebra		☐
10	decimals rates			algebra		☐
11	ratios		angles		data management	☐
12	percents rates				data management	☐
13	percents			algebra		☐
14	rates	measurement				☐
15	percents				data management	☐
16		measurement	Cartesian coordinate plane			☐
17		measurement	Cartesian coordinate plane		probability	☐
18	factors			algebra		☐
19	ratios		angles			☐
20		measurement	Cartesian coordinate plane			☐

ISBN: 978-1-77149-205-8

① Leslie has 2 photos that have the same area. One of the photos is a rectangle with a length of 15.68 cm and a width of 12.5 cm. The other photo is a square. What is the perimeter of the square photo?

Area of the rectangular photo: _____ × _____ = _____

Side length of the square photo: $\sqrt{}$ = _____

Perimeter of the square photo: _____ × 4 = _____

The perimeter of the square photo is _____ .

② Alyssa has saved $37.50 in nickels, dimes, and quarters. She has 4 times as many quarters as dimes and 2 times as many nickels as quarters. What fraction of Alyssa's money is in quarters?

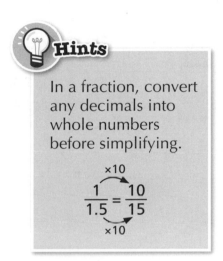

Hints

In a fraction, convert any decimals into whole numbers before simplifying.

×10

$$\frac{1}{1.5} = \frac{10}{15}$$

×10

③ Three streets intersect as shown. Robert found the ratios of the angles that Pine Street and Maple Street make with Oak Street as given in the diagram. What is c?

*not drawn to scale

Pine Street

Maple Street

c

a b d e

Oak Street

$a{:}b = 3{:}2$ $d{:}e = 4{:}5$

Topics covered:

Question 1
• square roots
• measurement

Question 2
• fractions
• decimals
• algebra

Question 3
• ratios
• angles

ISBN: 978-1-77149-205-8

④ Agnes has 2 square tiles to choose from for tiling a square shower stall floor. What is the smallest possible area of the floor if it can be tiled by either kind of square tile? How many more small tiles than big tiles are needed?

144 cm²

225 cm²

⑤ Chris has 3 cards labelled -5, -2, and 3. He randomly picks 1 card, puts it back, and then randomly picks another. If he multiplies the numbers on the cards he picks, what is the probability that he will get a product that is less than -5?

Hints

Use a tree diagram or a table to find the outcomes.

⑥ Kaitlyn wants to paint the outside of an open box. One can has 2.4 L of paint and 2 mL of paint covers 10 cm² of a surface. How many cans of paint will Kaitlyn use?

60 cm

40 cm

75 cm

Topics covered:

Question 4	**Question 5**	**Question 6**
• multiples	• integers	• decimals
• square roots	• probability	• measurement
• measurement		

ISBN: 978-1-77149-205-8

⑦ The ratio of length to width to height of Edward's old fish tank was 4:3:6. Each edge of his new fish tank is 50% longer than the old tank. What is the capacity of Edward's new fish tank if the width of his old fish tank was 18 cm?

⑧ Ryan and Ashley both flipped to a page of a 240-page book randomly. What was the probability that they both flipped to a page number that is a perfect square?

⑨ Each year, the fish population of a fish farm increased by $\frac{3}{4}$. After 2 years, the fish farm had 245 fish. What was the original fish population?

⑩ At a sugar factory, Machine A pours 3.41 kg of sugar into a tank every 5.5 s while Machine B removes 1.71 kg of sugar every 4.5 s from the tank for packaging. If the tank can hold 180 kg of sugar at most, how many seconds will it take for the tank to be full?

Topics covered:

Question 7	Question 8	Question 9	Question 10
• percents	• perfect squares	• fractions	• decimals
• ratios	• probability	• algebra	• rates
• measurement			• algebra

ISBN: 978-1-77149-205-8

⑪ Cathy's ice cream store sells 5 different flavours. She used a circle graph to track the monthly sales. She also noted the following:

- The sales from the vanilla, lemon, and mint flavours were half of the total sales.

- The ratio of lemon to mint ice cream sold was 1:2.

- The sales from the strawberry and mint flavours were the same.

72 vanilla flavoured ice cream cones were sold. How many chocolate flavoured ice cream cones were sold?

Monthly Ice Cream Sales

vanilla, strawberry, and chocolate

lemon and mint

⑫ Refer to Question 11. The price of each flavour is shown. What percent of the revenue came from the sales of the chocolate and vanilla flavours?

Price List

Chocolate Vanilla Strawberry	$5.50/cone
Lemon Mint	$6.25/cone

Topics covered:

Question 11	**Question 12**
• ratios	• percents
• angles	• rates
• data management	• data management

ISBN: 978-1-77149-205-8

⑬ John deposited $2000 into a simple interest savings account. After 2 years, he had $2200 in total. What was the annual interest rate?

⑭ It takes 1 worker 1 hour to dig a hole that is 2 m by 3 m by 4 m. How many hours are needed for 2 workers to dig a hole that is 1.5 m by 6 m by 8 m?

⑮ The average of Roy's first 5 test scores was 78%. He wants to raise his average to 80%. If his 6th test is scored out of 20 marks, how many marks must he get out of 20?

Topics covered:

Question 13	**Question 14**	**Question 15**
• percents	• rates	• percents
• algebra	• measurement	• data management

ISBN: 978-1-77149-205-8

⑯ Richard's farm is in the shape of a trapezoid. Its corners are at (-4,-3), (-1,3), (2,3), and (5,-3). Draw the farm on the grid and find its area.

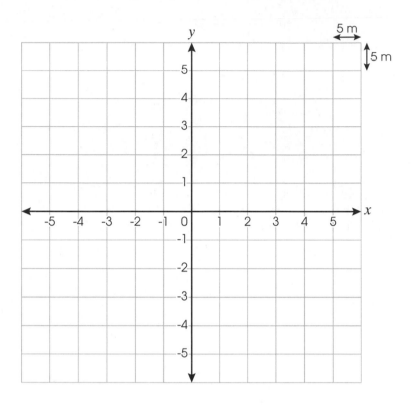

⑰ Refer to Question 16. Richard built a fence to fence his farm. His dog buried two bones where the grid lines intersect on the farm but not along the fence. There are 28 possible locations to hide the bones. What is the probability that both bones are in Quadrant IV if they can both be at the same location?

Hints

The points on either the *x*-axis or the *y*-axis do not belong to any quadrants.

Topics covered:

Question 16
• measurement
• Cartesian coordinate plane

Question 17
• measurement
• Cartesian coordinate plane
• probability

ISBN: 978-1-77149-205-8

⑱ A TV channel is airing a 36-min comedy and a 48-min drama back to back. There is a commercial break after airing a fixed number of minutes for each program, as well as between the programs. If the total airtime of both programs is 1 h 36 min, how long is each commercial break at most?

Hints

Find the GCF of 36 and 48 to help you solve the problem.

⑲ Elaine has a trapezoid that she wants to extend into a triangle as shown. She knows that ∠DBA and ∠BAC have a ratio of 2:1. What would the size of the extended angle, ∠BOD, be?

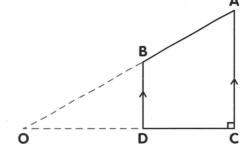

⑳ Peter translated the triangle shown so that the translated Point A is at (-3,-1). What are the coordinates of the vertices of the image? What is the area of the section where the triangle and its image overlap?

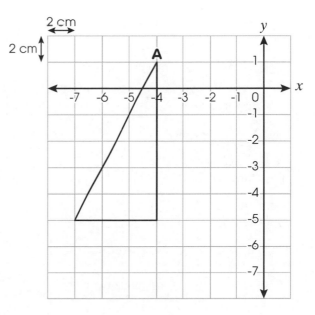

Topics covered:

Question 18	Question 19	Question 20
• factors	• ratios	• measurement
• algebra	• angles	• Cartesian coordinate plane

Students are required to solve multi-step questions which involve various topics in each.

ISBN: 978-1-77149-205-8

Topics Covered

	Number Sense and Numeration	Measurement	Geometry and Spatial Sense	Patterning and Algebra	Data Management and Probability	My Record ✔ correct ✘ incorrect
1	fractions rates	measurement				
2	decimals percents			algebra		
3	perfect squares decimals/ratios					
4	rates				data management	
5	fractions	measurement				
6	decimals			algebra		
7	square roots	measurement				
8	factors				probability	
9			angles	algebra		
10	decimals	measurement		algebra		
11	integers				data management	
12	integers			algebra		
13	ratios		angles			
14	decimals percents			algebra		
15	square roots	measurement		algebra		
16		measurement	Cartesian coordinate plane			
17			Cartesian coordinate plane		probability	
18	square roots ratios	measurement				
19	perfect squares		angles			
20	multiples rates					

① Tiffany mows a lawn that is in the shape of a trapezoid as shown in $6\frac{2}{3}$ min. What is her rate in m²/min?

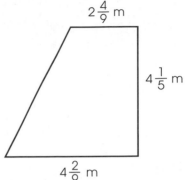

Area: (_____ + _____) × _____ ÷ 2

= _____

Rate: _____ ÷ _____ = _____

Tiffany's rate is _____ .

② Cassie has a 50-mL smoothie of milk and ice cream. 80% of it is ice cream. How much milk should be added so that the smoothie contains 25% of ice cream?

Hints

Think about how much ice cream is in the smoothie first. Then set up an equation.

③ A piece of 256-cm ribbon is cut into 3 pieces. The lengths of the three pieces are in the ratio of 5:6:9. The shortest piece is wrapped around the border of a square lid once. What is the area of the lid?

Topics covered:

Question 1	Question 2	Question 3
• fractions	• decimals	• perfect squares
• rates	• percents	• decimals
• measurement	• algebra	• ratios

ISBN: 978-1-77149-205-8

④ Erica went on a trip. She drove 4 hours at 95 km/h and 3 hours at 102 km/h. What were her mean and median speeds?

⑤ A cardboard box is $\frac{1}{2}$ m long, $\frac{1}{4}$ m wide, and its height is the sum of its length and width. What is the surface area of the cardboard box?

⑥ John has $5.65 in 25 coins that are dimes and quarters. How many of each kind of coin does he have?

Hints

If there are x dimes, the number of quarters will be $(25 - x)$.

⑦ The area of a cube's base is 169 cm². What is the volume of a stack of 6 cubes?

Topics covered:

Question 4	**Question 5**	**Question 6**	**Question 7**
• rates	• fractions	• decimals	• square roots
• data management	• measurement	• algebra	• measurement

ISBN: 978-1-77149-205-8

⑧ Jeff randomly picks a number from 1 to 20 and Sam randomly picks a number from 1 to 12. What is the probability that both pick a number that is a common factor of 12 and 20?

⑨ Arthur has drawn 2 lines that are perpendicular to each other and that intersect with a pair of parallel lines. Arthur knows that the measures of *a* and *b* are the same. What are the measures of *a* and *b*?

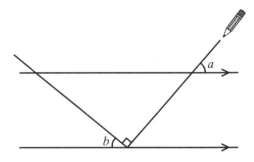

⑩ Chloe's prism has a volume of 50.4 cm³. What is the length of the longer base, *b*?

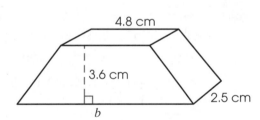

Topics covered:

Question 8	**Question 9**	**Question 10**
• factors	• angles	• decimals
• probability	• algebra	• measurement
		• algebra

ISBN: 978-1-77149-205-8

⑪ Simone recorded the temperatures of two cities last week in the double line graph. How much warmer was the mean temperature of Toronto than Calgary's?

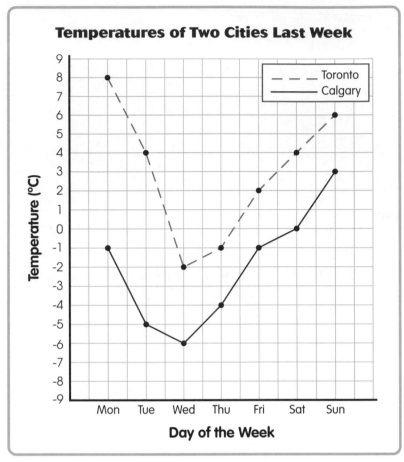

⑫ Refer to Question 11. Simone says, "Half of the mean temperature of Yellowknife last week was 4 times the sum of twice of Calgary's mean temperature and half of Toronto's mean temperature." What was the mean temperature of Yellowknife last week?

Topics covered:

Question 11	**Question 12**
• integers	• integers
• data management	• algebra

ISBN: 978-1-77149-205-8

⑬ Priscilla walked along the path from B to D. Is it possible to find the distance she walked? If so, what was it?

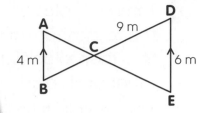

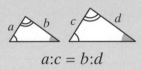

The corresponding sides of two triangles have the same ratio if their corresponding angles are the same.

$a{:}c = b{:}d$

⑭ Janice went shopping and bought a $40.50 shirt at 20% off and a $56 dress at 15% off. She paid a total of $88. What percent of tax did Janice pay?

Hints

The sales tax was applied on the discounted prices.

⑮ The surface area of a cube is 864 cm². Write an equation to find the side length of the cube.

Tips

$\sqrt{x^2} = x$

Topics covered:

Question 13	**Question 14**	**Question 15**
• ratios	• decimals	• square roots
• angles	• percents	• measurement
	• algebra	• algebra

ISBN: 978-1-77149-205-8

Tammy places a fence post at (-5,-5). She then places the other posts at:

- its reflection in the *y*-axis.
- 10 units up from it.
- its $\frac{1}{2}$ rotation about (0,0).

What is the area enclosed in Quadrant III?

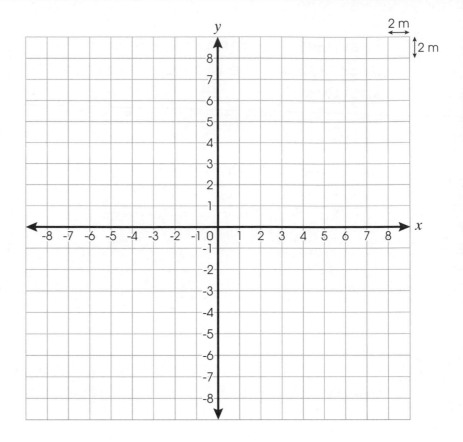

⑰ Refer to Question 16. A birdfeeder will be hung on the fence. What is the probability that it will be hung in Quadrant III?

**Hints**

Find the perimeter of the shape first.

Topics covered:

Question 16
- measurement
- Cartesian coordinate plane

Question 17
- Cartesian coordinate plane
- probability

ISBN: 978-1-77149-205-8

⑱   Amber is making a wedding cake with 3 square-based prisms. The height of each layer is 5 cm. The ratio of the side lengths of the square bases is 5:7:9. If the base area of the second layer is 196 cm², what is the volume of the entire cake?

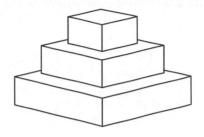

⑲   Are the angles in a regular decagon (a polygon with 10 equal sides and angles) perfect squares?

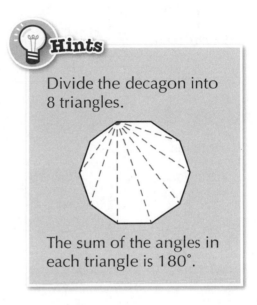

Hints

Divide the decagon into 8 triangles.

The sum of the angles in each triangle is 180°.

⑳   Two toy cars are running on separate square tracks that start at the same point. If both cars run at the same speed of 15 cm/s, how long will it take for the cars to meet at the starting point 10 times after starting?

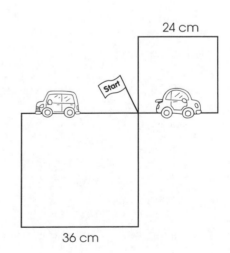

24 cm

Start

36 cm

Topics covered:

Question 18	**Question 19**	**Question 20**
• square roots	• perfect squares	• multiples
• ratios	• angles	• rates
• measurement		

ISBN: 978-1-77149-205-8

Students are required to solve multi-step questions which involve various topics in each.

Topics Covered

	Number Sense and Numeration	Measurement	Geometry and Spatial Sense	Patterning and Algebra	Data Management and Probability	My Record ✔ correct ✘ incorrect
1	decimals percents					☐
2	square roots	measurement				☐
3	percents			algebra		☐
4	decimals		angles			☐
5	ratios				probability	☐
6	fractions decimals			algebra		☐
7	decimals ratios	measurement				☐
8	percents				data management	☐
9					probability/data management	☐
10	rates			algebra	data management	☐
11	perfect squares		angles			☐
12	factors	measurement				☐
13	integers			algebra	data management	☐
14		measurement	Cartesian coordinate plane			☐
15	integers		Cartesian coordinate plane			☐
16	square roots	measurement				☐
17	fractions ratios					☐
18	multiples			algebra		☐
19	integers				probability	☐
20	ratios		angles			☐

ISBN: 978-1-77149-205-8

① Erica has ordered a sandwich that costs $12.40. There is a 13% sales tax.
If Erica pays an 18.5% tip after tax, how much change will she receive
after paying $20?

Cost after tax: _____ + _____ × _____ = _____

Cost after tip: _____ + _____ × _____ = _____

Change: $20 – _____ = _____

Erica will receive _____ in change.

② Trey painted a picture with an area of 169 cm². It is a parallelogram with
the same base and height. He added a border as shown. What is the
area of the border?

③ Andy had 50% of the candies that Woody had. Woody gave 20 candies
to Andy and they now have the same number of candies. How many
candies did Woody have originally?

Topics covered:

Question 1	**Question 2**	**Question 3**
• decimals	• square roots	• percents
• percents	• measurement	• algebra

ISBN: 978-1-77149-205-8

④ Tim thinks a is the largest angle out of all the angles in both triangles. Is he correct? If not, what is the size of the largest angle?

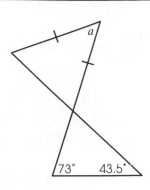

73°   43.5°

⑤ At a game booth, a player throws a token into one of the slots. The ratio of green to blue to red slots is 2:3:1. What is the probability of throwing a token into a red slot? About how many tokens have been thrown if 18 tokens are thrown into the red slots?

⑥ A juice bar sold a glass of apple juice for $5.25 and pineapple juice for $6.75. The total revenue was $441 and $\frac{1}{4}$ of it came from apple juice. How many glasses of juice were sold in total?

⑦ Wilson wants to wrap the gift shown. The bases of the trapezoid have a ratio of 1:2. How much wrapping paper is needed?

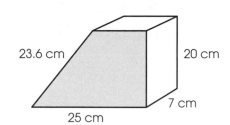

23.6 cm   20 cm

7 cm

25 cm

Topics covered:

Question 4	**Question 5**	**Question 6**	**Question 7**
• decimals	• ratios	• fractions	• decimals
• angles	• probability	• decimals	• ratios
		• algebra	• measurement

ISBN: 978-1-77149-205-8

⑧ The histogram shows the ages of the passengers on a flight. How many more passengers were younger than 30 than those who were older than 50 in percent?

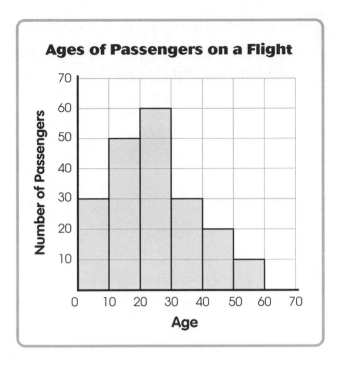

Ages of Passengers on a Flight

⑨ Refer to Question 8. 10% of the passengers on the flight sat in first class. If a passenger was picked at random, what was the probability that the passenger was one who sat in first class and was over 40 years old?

⑩ Refer to Question 9. The average ticket price was $1625/passenger. If a first class ticket cost $650 more than an economy ticket, how much did an economy ticket cost?

Topics covered:

Question 8
• percents
• data management

Question 9
• data management
• probability

Question 10
• rates
• algebra
• data management

⑪ All of the angles in a parallelogram are perfect squares that are greater than 15. What are the angles?

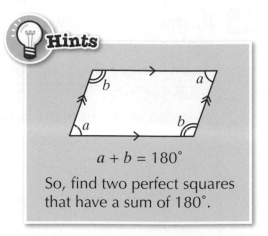

Hints

$a + b = 180°$

So, find two perfect squares that have a sum of 180°.

⑫ Snow globes are packaged in cube-shaped boxes. The cube-shaped boxes completely fill the cardboard box. At least how many snow globes are there in the box?

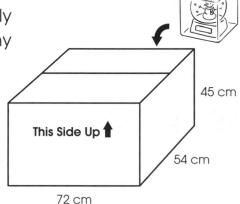

45 cm

This Side Up ⬆

54 cm

72 cm

⑬ The mean temperature from Monday to Wednesday was -2°C. The temperature decreased by 1°C from Monday to Tuesday, and increased by 5°C from Tuesday to Wednesday. What was the temperature on Monday?

Topics covered:

Question 11
• perfect squares
• angles

Question 12
• factors
• measurement

Question 13
• integers
• algebra
• data management

ISBN: 978-1-77149-205-8

⑭ 4 trees have been planted at the corner of a patio. The two old trees are at (-4,5) and (5,-2). The two new trees are at the reflection of the old trees in the *x*-axis. What is the area of the patio?

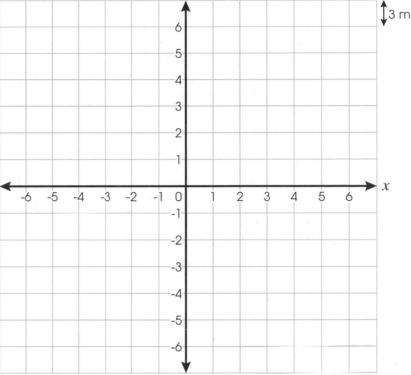

⑮ Refer to Question 14. Rachel tells her sister to find a treasure that she has hidden using the following clues.

- It is under the patio.
- It is in Quadrant II.
- The *x*- and *y*-coordinates have a sum of -3.

What are the coordinates of the treasure?

Topics covered:

Question 14
- measurement
- Cartesian coordinate plane

Question 15
- integers
- Cartesian coordinate plane

A square patio has a water fountain in the centre of it that takes up 5 m². The remaining area of the patio is 164 m². What is the perimeter of the patio?

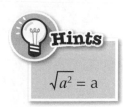

Hints

$$\sqrt{a^2} = a$$

⑰ The weights of tomatoes, cucumbers, and lettuce in a salad have a ratio of $1\frac{2}{3}$: $1\frac{5}{6}$: $1\frac{1}{2}$. If the total weight of the salad is 900 g, what is the weight of each ingredient?

⑱ Pencils are sold in boxes of 16 and erasers in boxes of 12. Larry has bought the least number of boxes so that the number of pencils and erasers are the same. He has used a total of 44 pencils and erasers and the number of erasers used is one third of the pencils used. How many pencils are left?

Topics covered:

Question 16	**Question 17**	**Question 18**
• square roots	• fractions	• multiples
• measurement	• ratios	• algebra

ISBN: 978-1-77149-205-8

⑲ Randall spins two wheels and finds the product of the two numbers. What is the probability of getting a negative product?

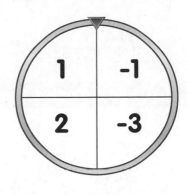

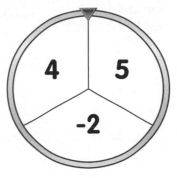

⑳ Mariah drew a triangle which had angles in a ratio of 3:2:1. She then drew lines to bisect each of those angles. What is a?

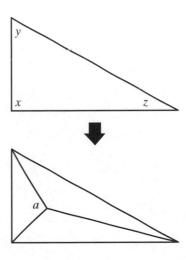

Topics covered:

Question 19
- integers
- probability

Question 20
- ratios
- angles

Students are required to solve multi-step questions which involve various topics in each.

Topics Covered

	Number Sense and Numeration	Measurement	Geometry and Spatial Sense	Patterning and Algebra	Data Management and Probability	My Record ✔ correct ✘ incorrect
1	rates	measurement				
2	multiples fractions					
3	percents			algebra		
4			angles		probability	
5	factors ratios					
6	fractions decimals			algebra		
7	integers perfect squares		Cartesian coordinate plane	algebra		
8	square roots	measurement	Cartesian coordinate plane			
9	decimals ratios					
10	fractions decimals	measurement				
11	percents			algebra		
12	fractions				data management	
13	fractions				data management	
14					probability/data management	
15	percents	measurement				
16	ratios		angles			
17	rates		Cartesian coordinate plane			
18	fractions			algebra	probability	
19	decimals percents			algebra		
20	fractions	measurement				

ISBN: 978-1-77149-205-8

① Janice is trying to find the cost of producing a juice box. A juice box is a square-based prism that measures 5 cm by 5 cm by 8 cm. The cardboard for the juice box costs $0.001/cm² and the juice costs $0.002/mL. What is the total cost of producing a juice box?

Surface area: _____ × _____ × 2 + _____ × _____ × 4

= _____

Cost of cardboard: _____ × _____ = _____

Volume: _____ × _____ × _____ = _____

Cost of juice: _____ × _____ = _____

Total cost: _____ + _____ = _____

The total cost of producing a juice box is _____ .

② The first bell rings every $\frac{1}{3}$ hour. The second bell rings every $\frac{3}{5}$ hour. The third bell rings every $\frac{2}{5}$ hour. If all three bells ring at 10:00 a.m., when will they all ring together again?

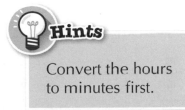

Hints

Convert the hours to minutes first.

③ Erin invested $4500 at a simple interest rate. If she has $4950 after 5 years, what was the simple interest rate?

Topics covered:

Question 1
• rates
• measurement

Question 2
• multiples
• fractions

Question 3
• percents
• algebra

ISBN: 978-1-77149-205-8

④ Three streets make the two intersections and Cars X and Y are at the intersections as shown. If each car makes a left turn, what is the probability that the sizes of the angles of both turns are the same?

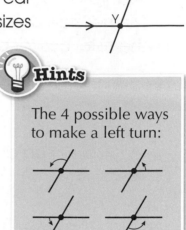

Hints

The 4 possible ways to make a left turn:

⑤ 360 kg of beads will be dyed red, blue, and green in a ratio of 2:3:10. If the beads of each colour will be packaged into a number of bags of equal weight, how many kilograms of beads will there be in each bag at most?

⑥ Daisy has 15 coins. She has 5 more loonies than quarters and $\frac{3}{4}$ as many loonies as toonies. How much money does Daisy have?

Topics covered:

Question 4	Question 5	Question 6
• angles	• factors	• fractions
• probability	• ratios	• decimals
		• algebra

ISBN: 978-1-77149-205-8

⑦ The city of Townsville has built three radio towers. They are located at the points below.

$X(\frac{b}{c}, abc)$

$Y(a + b, 3b)$

$Z(a + b^3, a)$

where $a = -1$, $b = 2$, and $c = -2$

What are the locations of the three radio towers? Plot them on the grid.

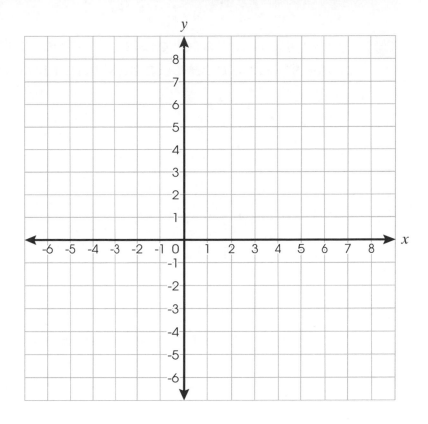

⑧ Refer to Question 7. The area of the triangle created by the radio towers is 832 km². What is the side length of each square on the grid?

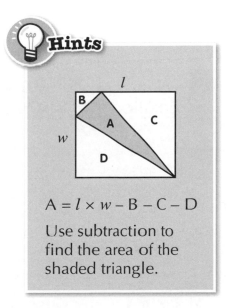

$A = l \times w - B - C - D$

Use subtraction to find the area of the shaded triangle.

Topics covered:

Question 7
- integers
- perfect squares
- Cartesian coordinate plane
- algebra

Question 8
- square roots
- measurement
- Cartesian coordinate plane

ISBN: 978-1-77149-205-8

⑨ Andy who is 1.5 m tall casts a 0.7-m long shadow. What would the length of the shadow cast by a skyscraper that is 100.5 m tall be?

Hints

The ratio of the height of the skyscraper to its shadow is the same as Andy's.

⑩ Amy wants to wrap a big gift that is $\frac{1}{3}$ m high, 1.2 m long, and $\frac{3}{4}$ m wide. What is the area of the wrapping paper she needs?

⑪ Vanessa has 240 mL of a solution that is 30% syrup. She wants to create a solution that is 40% syrup. How much syrup should she add?

Hints

Set up an equation with the same amount of syrup on both sides.

Topics covered:

Question 9	**Question 10**	**Question 11**
• decimals	• fractions	• percents
• ratios	• decimals	• algebra
	• measurement	

ISBN: 978-1-77149-205-8

⑫ Tegan did a survey on the movies people watched and created a circle graph. $\frac{3}{4}$ of the people who watched "The Forest Book" liked the movie. What fraction of the people surveyed who watched "The Forest Book" liked the movie?

Movies People Watched

⑬ Refer to Question 12. If 300 people watched "Decoy Prime", how many more people watched "Finding Dora" than "Urban Battle"?

⑭ Refer to Question 13. $\frac{1}{3}$ of the people who watched "Wild Borough" liked the movie. What was the probability that someone surveyed liked "Wild Borough"?

Topics covered:

Question 12	**Question 13**	**Question 14**
• fractions	• fractions	• data management
• data management	• data management	• probability

ISBN: 978-1-77149-205-8

⑮ Florence cut a block of butter that measured 12 cm by 4 cm by 4 cm. If 20% of the butter was cut, what is the surface area of the remaining block of butter?

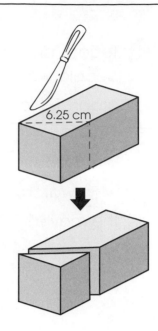

⑯ Adam drew 4 lines that make a quadrilateral. If *a*, *b*, *c*, and *d* are in a ratio of 4:3:6:2, what is the size of each angle in the quadrilateral?

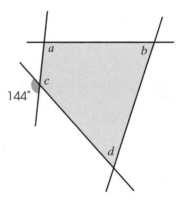

⑰ Mikayla is located at (5,6) on a grid. Each square on the grid has a length of 250 m. If she moves 200 m/min to the left and 100 m/min down, what will her location be after moving for 10 min in each direction?

Topics covered:		
Question 15	**Question 16**	**Question 17**
• percents	• ratios	• rates
• measurement	• angles	• Cartesian coordinate plane

ISBN: 978-1-77149-205-8

⑱ Liam has a deck of 10 cards that are red, blue, or black. There are 3 red cards. Liam says, "If I pick 2 cards with replacement each time, the probability of picking a red card and then a blue card is $\frac{3}{20}$." How many black cards are there?

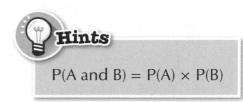

Hints

$$P(A \text{ and } B) = P(A) \times P(B)$$

⑲ Michael bought a shirt that was 50% off, plus an additional 20% off. If the discounted price before tax was $6.24, how much money did he save?

⑳ Katherine has built a tent that has the given dimensions. What is the volume of the tent?

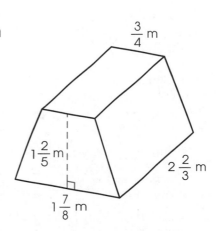

$\frac{3}{4}$ m

$1\frac{2}{5}$ m

$2\frac{2}{3}$ m

$1\frac{7}{8}$ m

Topics covered:

Question 18	**Question 19**	**Question 20**
• fractions	• decimals	• fractions
• algebra	• percents	• measurement
• probability	• algebra	

ISBN: 978-1-77149-205-8

Students are required to solve multi-step questions which involve various topics in each.

Topics Covered

	Number Sense and Numeration	Measurement	Geometry and Spatial Sense	Patterning and Algebra	Data Management and Probability	My Record ✔ correct ✘ incorrect
1	factors square roots	measurement				☐
2	fractions			algebra	probability	☐
3	integers percents					☐
4	multiples/factors perfect squares					☐
5		measurement		algebra		☐
6	square roots ratios				probability	☐
7	decimals percents			algebra		☐
8	integers				probability	☐
9	ratios		angles			☐
10	fractions/decimals percents					☐
11	perfect squares integers		Cartesian coordinate plane	algebra		☐
12	fractions		Cartesian coordinate plane			☐
13	square roots	measurement				☐
14	fractions				probability	☐
15	fractions ratios	measurement				☐
16	fractions percents				data management	☐
17	fractions percents				data management	☐
18	perfect squares	measurement		algebra		☐
19		ratios	angles			☐
20	fractions percents			algebra		☐

ISBN: 978-1-77149-205-8

① Jessie has 2 square pieces of paper that are 144 cm² and 256 cm². She wants to cut them into the biggest possible identical squares with no left over. What is the perimeter of each cut square? How many squares will be made?

GCF of 144 and 256: _____

Side length of cut squares: $\sqrt{\underline{\hspace{1cm}}}$ = _____

Perimeter of cut squares: _____ × 4 = _____

No. of cut squares: 144 ÷ _____ + 256 ÷ _____ = _____

The perimeter of each cut square is _____ . _____ squares will be made.

② There are 7 more boys than girls in Mr. Cheung's class. $\frac{2}{5}$ of the boys and $\frac{3}{4}$ of the girls were born in Toronto. If the numbers of boys and girls born in Toronto are the same, how many girls are there? If one of the students won a contest, what is the probability that the student is a girl?

③ The temperature yesterday was -18°C. If today's temperature is 80% of yesterday's temperature, what is the change in temperature?

Topics covered:

Question 1	Question 2	Question 3
• factors	• fractions	• integers
• square roots	• algebra	• percents
• measurement	• probability	

④ 36 is the LCM of two perfect squares. What are the perfect squares other than 1 and 36?

Hints

Express 36 as a product of prime numbers.

⑤ A door has a window. The door is three times as wide as the window. The widths of both the window and the door are half of their own heights. If the total area of the door is 11 250 cm², what is the area of the window?

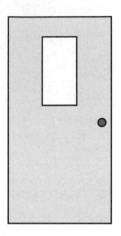

⑥ Shauna has red marbles and blue marbles in a bag. She picks 2 marbles with replacement each time. If the probability of picking 2 red marbles is $\frac{1}{4}$, in what ratio are the red marbles to blue marbles?

⑦ Amanda puts $670 into her bank account, from which she earns a 7% simple interest semi-annually. How many years will it take her to have $1045.20?

Hints

"Semi-annually" means twice a year.

Topics covered:

Question 4	**Question 5**	**Question 6**	**Question 7**
• multiples	• measurement	• square roots	• decimals
• factors	• algebra	• ratios	• percents
• perfect squares		• probability	• algebra

ISBN: 978-1-77149-205-8

⑧ Perry and Mary both roll 6-sided dice. The dice are labelled 1 to 6. Perry subtracts the number he rolls from Mary's number. What is the probability that the number is less than -2?

Use a table to find all the possible outcomes.

⑨ Veronica drew a quadrilateral. She found that *d*:*a* is 3:5 and *c*:*b* is 3:2. What is the size of each angle?

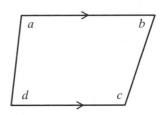

*not drawn to scale

⑩ Laura's old water bottle can hold 1.28 L. Her new water bottle can hold 30% more. If Laura's new bottle is $\frac{7}{8}$ full, how much water is there?

Topics covered:

Question 8	**Question 9**	**Question 10**
• integers	• ratios	• fractions
• probability	• angles	• decimals
		• percents

⑪ Leon is telling Jill his location using these clues. He says,

- "Two units to the right of my x-coordinate is three times two units to the left of my x-coordinate."

- "5 units down from the square of your y-coordinate is equal to my y-coordinate divided by -3."

Where is Leon? In which quadrant is he?

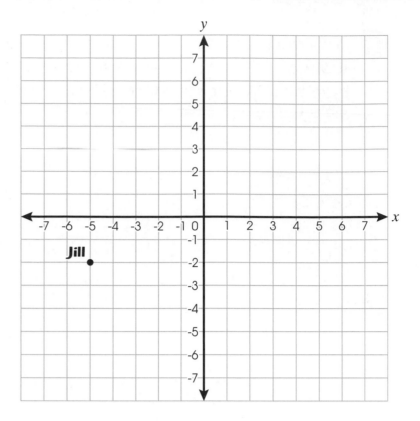

⑫ Refer to Question 11. To walk toward Leon, Jill takes the shortest path, changing her direction only once. If she meets Ivan $\frac{5}{7}$ of the way, what are Ivan's possible locations?

There are two possible positions.

Topics covered:

Question 11
- perfect squares
- integers
- Cartesian coordinate plane
- algebra

Question 12
- fractions
- Cartesian coordinate plane

ISBN: 978-1-77149-205-8

⑬ Stephen cut out a square-based prism out of a 12-cm cube. If the remaining solid has a volume of 1536 cm³, what is the surface area of the cut-out?

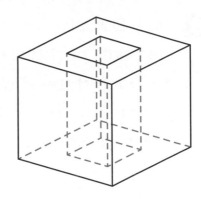

⑭ Mark subscribes to a magazine program which will send him 1 magazine each month. In the program, $\frac{1}{3}$ of the possible magazines are fashion magazines, $\frac{1}{5}$ are travel magazines, and the rest are sports magazines. What is the probability that Mark will receive 2 issues of sports magazines in two consecutive months?

⑮ The corresponding side lengths of the 2 right triangles shown are in the ratio of $1:1\frac{2}{3}$. They are combined to form the trapezoid. What are the area and perimeter of the trapezoid?

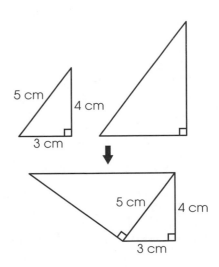

5 cm 4 cm 3 cm

5 cm 4 cm 3 cm

Topics covered:

Question 13
• square roots
• measurement

Question 14
• fractions
• probability

Question 15
• fractions
• ratios
• measurement

ISBN: 978-1-77149-205-8

⑯ Mr. Daniel has recorded the percent of painting completed for each student in the histogram. Robert has completed $\frac{3}{4}$ of his painting. How many other students are in the same range as Robert?

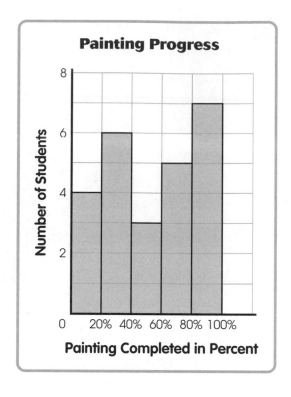

Painting Progress

Number of Students

Painting Completed in Percent

⑰ Refer to Question 16. Mr. Daniel estimates that it takes 1 hour for each student to complete a painting. How much more time should Mr. Daniel give his students if he wants at least 48% of them to complete their paintings?

Hints

Find out how much time the top 48% of the students need.

Topics covered:

Question 16
- fractions
- percents
- data management

Question 17
- fractions
- percents
- data management

ISBN: 978-1-77149-205-8

⑱ Patrick constructs a rectangular prism in which the length is the square of the height and the width is the square root of the length. If the volume of the prism is 16 cm³, what is its surface area?

$2^2 = 4$
$2^3 = 8$
$2^4 = 16$
⋮

⑲ The diagram shows the intersections and their angles. What is the ratio of x to y to z?

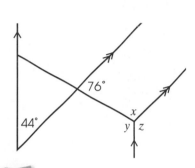

The sum of the angles around a point is 360°.

⑳ Frank's bookshelf has 20 science fiction, mystery, and fantasy novels. There are $\frac{1}{6}$ as many science fiction novels as mystery novels and $\frac{1}{2}$ as many fantasy novels as mystery novels. What percent of the novels are fantasy novels?

Topics covered:

Question 18
- perfect squares
- measurement
- algebra

Question 19
- ratios
- angles

Question 20
- fractions
- percents
- algebra

ISBN: 978-1-77149-205-8

Students are required to solve multi-step questions which involve various topics in each.

Topics Covered

	Number Sense and Numeration	Measurement	Geometry and Spatial Sense	Patterning and Algebra	Data Management and Probability	My Record ✔ correct ✘ incorrect
1	square roots decimals	measurement				☐
2	percents			algebra		☐
3	factors perfect squares				probability	☐
4	decimals ratios	measurement		algebra		☐
5	fractions		angles	algebra		☐
6	multiples square roots					☐
7	integers decimals				data management	☐
8	ratios			algebra		☐
9	decimals percents			algebra		☐
10	fractions rates					☐
11	decimals		Cartesian coordinate plane			☐
12		measurement	Cartesian coordinate plane			☐
13	fractions decimals			algebra		☐
14	perfect squares		angles			☐
15	factors				probability	☐
16	integers				data management	☐
17	integers percents				data management	☐
18	ratios	measurement				☐
19	decimals			algebra		☐
20		measurement			probability	☐

ISBN: 978-1-77149-205-8

① A sheet of metal is 55.8 cm long and 33.4 cm wide. A square with an area of 49 cm^2 is cut from each corner. The sheet is then folded into a box. What is the capacity of the box in millilitres?

② Donald is making fruit punch. 50% of the 1-L fruit punch is from juice concentrate. How much water should he add to the fruit punch so that it has 20% juice concentrate instead?

③ Kenneth rolls 2 dice that are labelled 1 to 6. What is the probability that the sum of the numbers is not a perfect square but a factor of 24?

Topics covered:

Question 1
- square roots
- decimals
- measurement

Question 2
- percents
- algebra

Question 3
- factors
- perfect squares
- probability

④ A school zone that is in the shape of a parallelogram is composed of a triangular lawn and a parking lot. The area of the lawn is 384 m² and its height is $\frac{4}{3}$ of its base. What is the ratio of the area of the lawn to the area of the parking lot?

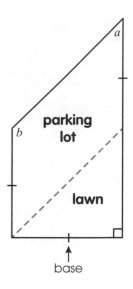

⑤ Refer to Question 4. The size of b is $3\frac{4}{9}$ times that of a. What are the sizes of the angles in the triangular lawn?

⑥ Farmer Tyler fenced a square piece of land that has an area of 576 m². Posts were added to strengthen the fencing. If the numbers of posts on the four sides of the fencing are the same, should the posts be 5 m apart or 8 m apart?

Topics covered:

Question 4
• decimals
• ratios
• measurement
• algebra

Question 5
• fractions
• angles
• algebra

Question 6
• multiples
• square roots

ISBN: 978-1-77149-205-8

⑦ Rachel recorded the temperatures in the past week. What were the mean, median, and mode temperatures?

Temperatures in the Past Week

Day	Temperature (˚C)
Mon	0.7
Tue	-1.2
Wed	1.3
Thu	-2.2
Fri	-3.4
Sat	1.3
Sun	-0.7

⑧ A recipe makes a dozen cookies using butter, sugar, and flour. The ratio of butter to sugar is 1:2 and the amount of flour needed is 2.5 times the amount of sugar. If each cookie weighs 12 g, how much sugar is needed for the recipe?

⑨ The regular price of a scarf was $23. Connie paid $20.24 after a discount and a 10% tax. What was the discount in percent?

⑩ A plane and a helicopter left the same airport at 3:25 p.m. and travelled in opposite directions. The plane flew at 888 km/h and the helicopter at 156 km/h. If both landed at 6:15 p.m., how far apart were they?

Topics covered:

Question 7	Question 8	Question 9	Question 10
• integers	• ratios	• decimals	• fractions
• decimals	• algebra	• percents	• rates
• data management		• algebra	

ISBN: 978-1-77149-205-8

⑪ Marilyn was at the corner of a park which is at (4,-4). She walked 40.5 m up and 27 m to the left to reach another corner. Where is Marilyn now?

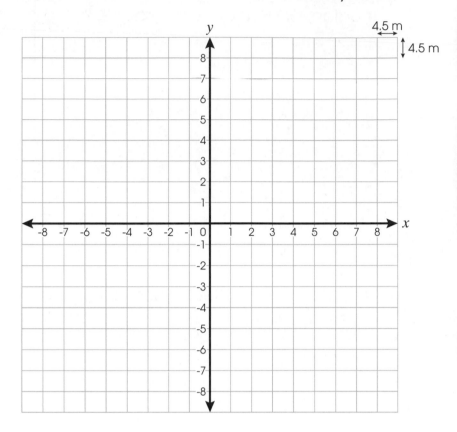

⑫ Refer to Question 11. The park is in the shape of a trapezoid and one of its corners is at (-6,5). If it has an area of 1275.75 m² and a height of 40.5 m, what are the coordinates of the last corner? Draw the park.

Topics covered:

Question 11
• decimals
• Cartesian coordinate plane

Question 12
• measurement
• Cartesian coordinate plane

ISBN: 978-1-77149-205-8

⑬ Corey was selling chocolate bars. He sold 95 chocolate bars during the weekdays. On the weekend, he sold $\frac{2}{5}$ of the remainder. In the end, he had 22% of the chocolate bars he started with. How many chocolate bars did he start with?

⑭ Billy says, "All of the angles in Triangle ABC are perfect squares." Is Billy correct?

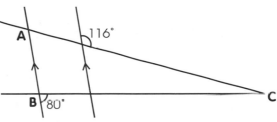

⑮ Raya had a blue ribbon that was 112 cm long and a red ribbon that was 84 cm long. She cut them into the longest possible pieces of equal lengths without leftovers. If she picks 2 pieces randomly with replacement each time, what is the probability of picking 2 blue ribbons?

Topics covered:

Question 13
- fractions
- decimals
- algebra

Question 14
- perfect squares
- angles

Question 15
- factors
- probability

ISBN: 978-1-77149-205-8

⑯ Chloe and Kimberly both began the year with $100. They compared the monthly change of their bank balances using a double line graph. What was the difference between their total bank balances at the end of May?

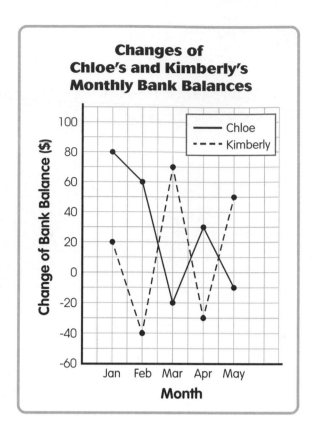

Changes of Chloe's and Kimberly's Monthly Bank Balances

⑰ Refer to Question 16. Chloe's change of bank balance in June was -$40. What was Kimberly's change of bank balance in June if her total bank balance at the end of June was 40% of Chloe's?

Topics covered:

Question 16
- integers
- data management

Question 17
- integers
- percents
- data management

ISBN: 978-1-77149-205-8

⑱ A square yard is divided into 3 sections. Sections x and z have the same area and the ratio of $\overline{BC}$ to $\overline{CD}$ is 2:1. What is the area of Section y?

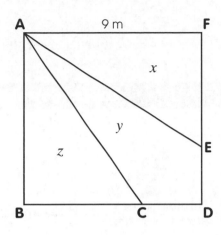

⑲ Edward has collected 28 stamps. Each one is worth 55¢, $1, or $1.25. The number of 55¢ stamps is half the number of $1.25 stamps. If the total value of his stamps is $28.20, how many $1.25 stamps does he have?

⑳ Ronald spins two wheels to determine the base and height of a triangle that he will draw. What is the probability that the area of the triangle is less than 10 cm²?

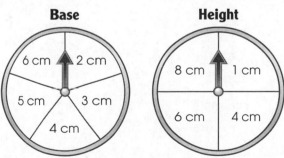

Topics covered:

Question 18
• ratios
• measurement

Question 19
• decimals
• algebra

Question 20
• measurement
• probability

ISBN: 978-1-77149-205-8

Students are required to solve multi-step questions which involve various topics in each.

Topics Covered

	Number Sense and Numeration	Measurement	Geometry and Spatial Sense	Patterning and Algebra	Data Management and Probability	My Record ✔ correct ✘ incorrect
1	square roots ratios	measurement				
2	multiples			algebra		
3	fractions percents					
4	ratios				probability	
5			angles	algebra		
6	decimals rates	measurement				
7	factors perfect squares					
8	fractions decimals			algebra		
9	percents				data management	
10	percents ratios	measurement				
11	percents		Cartesian coordinate plane			
12	rates		Cartesian coordinate plane			
13	perfect squares integers				probability	
14	fractions	measurement		algebra		
15			angles	algebra		
16	percents				data management	
17					probability/data management	
18	decimals percents	measurement				
19	perfect squares		angles			
20	fractions			algebra	probability	

ISBN: 978-1-77149-205-8

① Bruno cuts a square piece of paper that has an area of 625 cm² into 2 identical trapezoids. The bases of each trapezoid has a ratio of 1:4. How long are the bases?

② Mary set 2 stop watches. One rang every 2 minutes and the other rang every 5 minutes. She started them at 8:00 a.m. and stopped them after they rang a total of 35 times. If both watches were ringing when they were stopped, when did she stop the watches? How many times did the watches ring together?

③ Mom baked a batch of cookies. Anna and Elsa each ate 32 cookies. Dad ate $\frac{1}{4}$ of the remainder. Mom finished the remaining cookies which were 15% of the total cookies she had baked. How many cookies did Mom bake?

Topics covered:

Question 1	**Question 2**	**Question 3**
• square roots	• multiples	• fractions
• ratios	• algebra	• percents
• measurement		

ISBN: 978-1-77149-205-8

④ At a charity event, blue and pink raffle tickets are sold. For blue tickets, the ratio of the number of winning tickets to all blue tickets is 1:10 and the ratio is 1:8 for pink tickets. If Sandy buys 1 blue ticket and 1 pink ticket, what is the probability that she will win both raffles?

⑤ Martha measured the angles in terms of x. What is the measure of w?

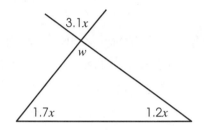

⑥ Alice bought a bar of soap in the shape of a trapezoidal prism. If the soap cost \$0.05/g and is 0.95 g/cm^3, how much did Alice pay?

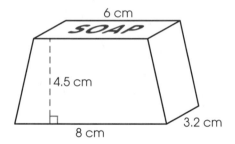

⑦ Boris says, "The GCF of 2 numbers is the same as the GCF of the squares of those numbers." Is he correct? If not, what is the relationship between the two GCFs?

Topics covered:

Question 4	**Question 5**	**Question 6**	**Question 7**
• ratios	• angles	• decimals	• factors
• probability	• algebra	• rates	• perfect squares
		• measurement	

ISBN: 978-1-77149-205-8

⑧ Ezra paid for a $8.75 lunch with a $50 bill. For change, he got $\frac{3}{2}$ as many $10 bills as $5 bills and $2\frac{1}{2}$ as many quarters as $5 bills. How many bills and coins did Ezra get back?

⑨ The scores of the students in Ms. Brown's class are as shown. What percent of the students scored higher than the mean score?

Students' Scores

No. of Students	Scores
2	52
9	74
7	80
3	84
4	92

⑩ The ratio of the length to width to height of Ken's box is 7:6:8. The width of the box is 3 dm. The dimensions of Erin's box are all 20% smaller than Ken's. How much greater is the volume of Ken's box than Erin's?

Topics covered:

Question 8
• fractions
• decimals
• algebra

Question 9
• percents
• data management

Question 10
• percents
• ratios
• measurement

ISBN: 978-1-77149-205-8

⑪ Ally began running at Point A along the path to Point B. What percent of her path was in each quadrant? What were the coordinates of Ally's location when she completed 65% of her path?

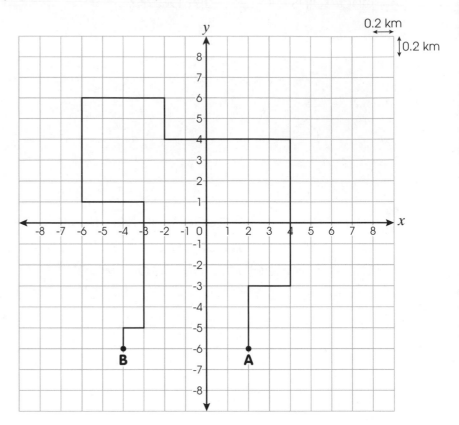

⑫ Refer to Question 11. Ally ran the path from 3:17 p.m. to 4:21 p.m. What was her speed? If she kept her speed, where would she be after running on the same path from Point B to Point A for 8 min?

Topics covered:

Question 11
- percents
- Cartesian coordinate plane

Question 12
- rates
- Cartesian coordinate plane

ISBN: 978-1-77149-205-8

⑬ Matthew has 5 cards with numbers as shown. He picks two cards with replacement each time and finds their product. Is it more likely to have a positive or a negative product? By how much in percent?

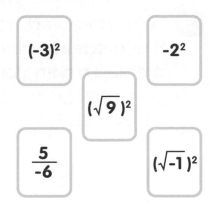

⑭ Kyle cut a wooden block into a triangular prism and a trapezoidal prism. If the volume of the triangular prism is $\frac{3}{5}$ of the volume of the trapezoidal prism, what is b?

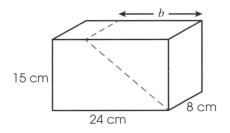

⑮ What are the measures of a, b and c?

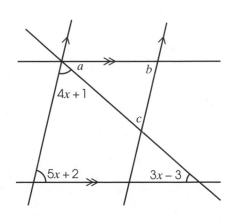

Topics covered:

Question 13
- perfect squares
- integers
- probability

Question 14
- fractions
- measurement
- algebra

Question 15
- angles
- algebra

ISBN: 978-1-77149-205-8

⑯ Sally collected some seashells. She measured their weights and created a histogram. What range of weights encompasses 12.5% of all seashells?

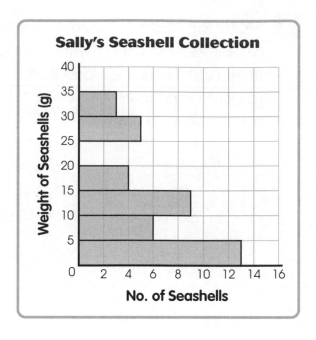

Sally's Seashell Collection

⑰ Refer to Question 16. Sally places all the seashells in a bag. If she picks two seashells with replacement each time, what is the probability that the first seashell is heavier than 25 g and the second seashell is lighter than 20 g?

Topics covered:

Question 16
- percents
- data management

Question 17
- data management
- probability

ISBN: 978-1-77149-205-8

⑱ Louis used 60% of his modelling clay to build a house as shown. What is the volume of the remaining modelling clay?

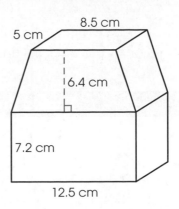

5 cm

8.5 cm

6.4 cm

7.2 cm

12.5 cm

⑲ Rylan says, "The sizes of the angles in a triangle can be 6^2, 8^2, and 9^2 degrees." Is Rylan correct?

⑳ Edward has a bag of 9 marbles. The number of red marbles is half as many as blue marbles. If Edward picks a marble from the bag 3 times with replacement each time, what is the probability of picking a red marble all 3 times?

Topics covered:

Question 18
- decimals
- percents
- measurement

Question 19
- perfect squares
- angles

Question 20
- fractions
- algebra
- probability

ISBN: 978-1-77149-205-8

Students are required to solve multi-step questions which involve various topics in each.

Topics Covered

	Number Sense and Numeration	Measurement	Geometry and Spatial Sense	Patterning and Algebra	Data Management and Probability	My Record ✔ correct ✗ incorrect
1	decimals			algebra		☐
2	fractions	measurement				☐
3	integers decimals				data management	☐
4	decimals		angles			☐
5	percents				data management	☐
6	multiples perfect squares	measurement				☐
7	rates			algebra		☐
8	percents		angles			☐
9	percents rates					☐
10	square roots decimals	measurement				☐
11	percents				data management	☐
12				algebra	data management	☐
13	percents ratios	measurement				☐
14	fractions percents			algebra		☐
15	fractions percents				probability	☐
16	ratios		Cartesian coordinate plane			☐
17		measurement	Cartesian coordinate plane			☐
18	percents rates					☐
19	fractions percents				data management	☐
20	multiples		angles			☐

ISBN: 978-1-77149-205-8

① Lana wants to hire someone to clean her house.   Melody charges $30 for the first 2 hours, plus $10.25 for each additional hour. Amy charges $28 for the first hour, plus $8.75 for each additional hour. At how many hours will Melody and Amy charge the same amount? Whom should Lana hire if she needs 7.8 hours of cleaning?

② A slice of cake is a triangular prism made up of 3 equal sections. What is the volume of the middle section?

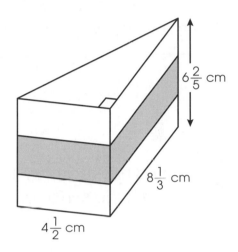

$6\frac{2}{5}$ cm

$8\frac{1}{3}$ cm

$4\frac{1}{2}$ cm

③ Mitch recorded the elevations of 4 different locations. What are the mean, median, and mode elevations of the locations?

Elevations of Different Locations

Location	Elevation (above/below sea level in metres)
1	-4.64
2	-1.32
3	0.96
4	3.12

Topics covered:

Question 1
• decimals
• algebra

Question 2
• fractions
• measurement

Question 3
• integers
• decimals
• data management

ISBN: 978-1-77149-205-8

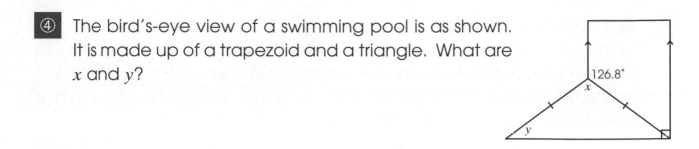

④ The bird's-eye view of a swimming pool is as shown. It is made up of a trapezoid and a triangle. What are x and y?

⑤ A bucket with a capacity of 30.2 L was used to collect rainwater. The mean amount of rainwater collected for the first two days was 18% of the bucket's capacity. The mean for the next four days was 12% of the bucket's capacity. If the bucket was filled on the 7th day, how much rainwater was collected that day?

⑥ David has rectangular prisms that measure 3 cm by 5 cm by 7 cm each. What is the surface area of the smallest cube that can be built with these prisms?

⑦ To print photos at Wellers, it costs $1.00 plus 22¢/photo. At SilverMart, it costs $3.40 plus 10¢/photo. For how many photos will the prices of printing be the same at both stores?

Topics covered:

Question 4	**Question 5**	**Question 6**	**Question 7**
• decimals	• percents	• multiples	• rates
• angles	• data management	• perfect squares	• algebra
		• measurement	

ISBN: 978-1-77149-205-8

⑧ △MQS is divided into shapes including 2 congruent triangles: △OPQ and △ONM. What percent of the triangles in △MQS are obtuse triangles? (There are 8 triangles in total.)

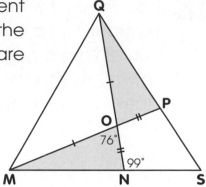

⑨ Brendan earned \$11.50/h and he is earning more after an 8% raise. If he used to work 27 hours a week, how many fewer hours does he work to earn the same as before?

⑩ Cammy had a square handkerchief with an area of 196 cm². She added a border to make it bigger with an area of 361 cm². What is the thickness of the added border?

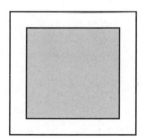

Topics covered:

Question 8
- percents
- angles

Question 9
- percents
- rates

Question 10
- square roots
- decimals
- measurement

ISBN: 978-1-77149-205-8

⑪ Rida recorded the colour of the scarves at her store and created a circle graph. If there were 85 more grey scarves than red scarves, how many scarves were there in total? How many scarves in each colour were there?

Colours of Scarves

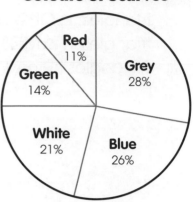

⑫ Refer to Question 11. Red, blue, and green scarves cost $2 more than white and grey scarves. If all the scarves cost $6000 altogether, how much did each colour of scarf cost?

Topics covered:

Question 11
- percents
- data management

Question 12
- algebra
- data management

ISBN: 978-1-77149-205-8

⑬ Charlie's birdhouse is a rectangular prism. The ratio of its width to length to height is 5:7:9. He has built a new birdhouse where each dimension is increased by 25%. If the length of his old birdhouse is 28 cm, what is the volume of his new birdhouse?

⑭ Ms. Wood's class had a bake sale. They sold 67% of the cookies on Wednesday and $\frac{1}{3}$ of the remainder on Thursday. All the remaining 66 cookies were shared amongst themselves. How many cookies did they sell in total?

⑮ Cough medicine must pass two tests before it can be sold. 97% of the bottles tested passed the first test. The second test had a failure rate of $\frac{1}{50}$. If 5000 bottles were tested, how many bottles passed both tests?

Topics covered:

Question 13	**Question 14**	**Question 15**
• percents	• fractions	• fractions
• ratios	• percents	• percents
• measurement	• algebra	• probability

ISBN: 978-1-77149-205-8

⑯ Molly's field is on the grid. (-4,2) is one of the corners of her rectangular field. If the width to length ratio of her field is 2:3, where are the other corners of the largest possible field?

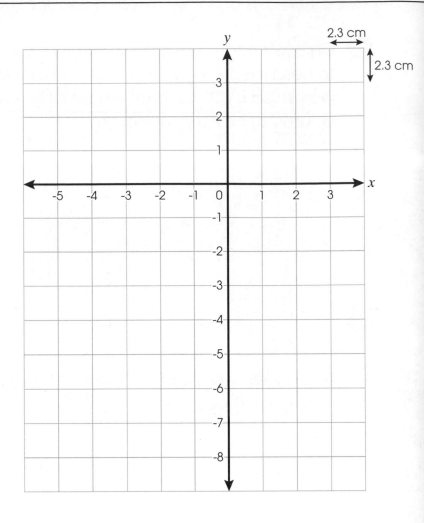

2.3 cm

2.3 cm

⑰ Refer to Question 16. What are the area and perimeter of the largest possible field?

Topics covered:

Question 16
- ratios
- Cartesian coordinate plane

Question 17
- measurement
- Cartesian coordinate plane

ISBN: 978-1-77149-205-8

⑱ An oxygen tank has a capacity of 250 L. It releases oxygen at a rate of 1.4 L/min. How long will it take for the tank to have 30% oxygen remaining?

⑲ The mean score of Andre's first 5 tests was 78%. His mean score increased to 79% after his 6th test and then dropped to 78% after his 7th test. If each test had 50 questions, how many of the questions did Andre answer correctly in his 6th and 7th tests?

⑳ Saul is describing Triangles A, B, or C. He says, "One of the angles is the LCM of the other two angles." Which triangle could Saul be describing?

Triangle A: an equilateral triangle

Triangle B: an obtuse triangle with angles of 45° and 36°

Triangle C: an isosceles triangle with two 80° angles

Topics covered:

Question 18	**Question 19**	**Question 20**
• percents	• fractions	• multiples
• rates	• percents	• angles
	• data management	

ISBN: 978-1-77149-205-8

Students are required to solve multi-step questions which involve various topics in each.

Topics Covered

	Number Sense and Numeration	Measurement	Geometry and Spatial Sense	Patterning and Algebra	Data Management and Probability	My Record ✔ correct ✗ incorrect
1	fractions ratios					☐
2			angles		probability	☐
3	factors	measurement				☐
4	percents			algebra		☐
5	decimals percents	measurement				☐
6	multiples perfect squares					☐
7	fractions		angles			☐
8	integers rates			algebra		☐
9	fractions/decimals percents			algebra		☐
10	percents rates					☐
11	percents				data management	☐
12	percents				probability/data management	☐
13	fractions decimals			algebra		☐
14	multiples	measurement				☐
15	square roots integers					☐
16	fractions decimals		Cartesian coordinate plane			☐
17		measurement	Cartesian coordinate plane			☐
18	square roots percents			algebra	probability	☐
19	ratios		angles			☐
20	fractions decimals	measurement				☐

ISBN: 978-1-77149-205-8

① There were 100 bananas and pears. The number of bananas to pears was in a ratio of 3:7. $\frac{2}{5}$ of the bananas and 25 pears were consumed. What is the ratio of bananas to pears now?

② "Socks", "Ruler", and "Pencil" make up half of the spinner. Amelia spins the wheel twice. What is the probability that she wins a ruler and a teddy bear?

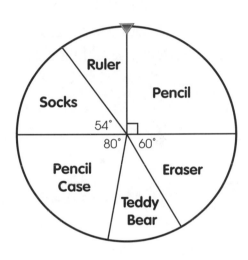

③ Megan wants to make a box that has a volume of 75 cm³ and a surface area of 190 cm². All the dimensions are whole numbers. What are the dimensions of the box?

④ Carly ordered a dish that cost $30. She got a 10% student discount. She tipped the same amount as the tax. If she paid $32.40 in total, what was the tax rate?

⑤ Fred plans to make a model of a speed bump by cutting a square-based prism out of a triangular prism as shown. What percent of the original prism will be cut? If the bump is to be painted except the bottom, what area needs to be painted?

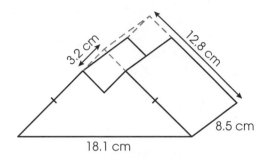

⑥ The LCM of 2 perfect squares is always a perfect square. Can 2 numbers that are not perfect squares have an LCM that is a perfect square? Give an example.

⑦ What are the sizes of the angles in Triangle ABC?

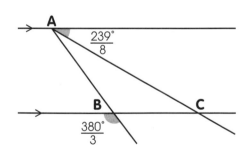

Topics covered:

Question 4	**Question 5**	**Question 6**	**Question 7**
• percents	• decimals	• multiples	• fractions
• algebra	• percents	• perfect squares	• angles
	• measurement		

ISBN: 978-1-77149-205-8

⑧ Mia and Marcus have initial savings of $40 and $96 respectively. Mia's savings are +$11.50/week and Marcus's are -$16.50/week. After how many weeks will they have the same amount of savings?

⑨ Matt baked a cake. He ate 12% of it and then gave $\frac{3}{4}$ of the remaining cake to his sister. If he has 0.572 kg of cake left, what was the weight of the original cake?

⑩ Darla is selling lemonade for $0.75/cup. She has spent $5.25 on ingredients. How many cups does she need to sell if she wants to make a revenue that is 300% greater than the money spent on ingredients?

Topics covered:

Question 8	Question 9	Question 10
• integers	• fractions	• percents
• rates	• decimals	• rates
• algebra	• percents	
	• algebra	

⑪ A building's management team kept track of the usage of elevators and stairs by its residents. The double line graph shows the data in percents. The mean usage of elevators from January to August was 70%. If the residents used either elevators or stairs, what was the usage of stairs in August?

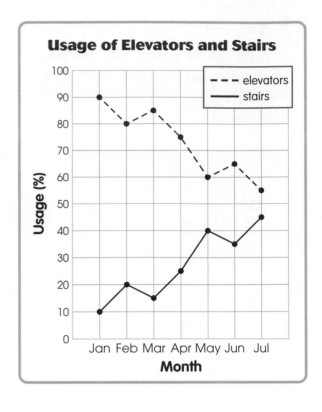

Usage of Elevators and Stairs

⑫ Refer to Question 11. For a family of 4, what was the probability that in May, 3 members of the family took the elevators and 1 member took the stairs?

Topics covered:

Question 11
• percents
• data management

Question 12
• percents
• data management
• probability

ISBN: 978-1-77149-205-8

⑬ Mona and Leo each have 12 coins in loonies and quarters only. Mona has twice as many quarters as Leo, but only $\frac{2}{3}$ of his money amount. How much does Leo have?

⑭ How many of the trapezoidal prisms shown are needed to completely fill the smallest possible cube-shaped box? What is the volume of the cube-shaped box?

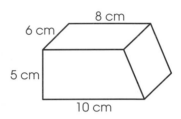

6 cm
8 cm
5 cm
10 cm

⑮ Leon thinks that $\sqrt{4}$ is equal to both 2 and -2. Is he correct?

Topics covered:

Question 13
- fractions
- decimals
- algebra

Question 14
- multiples
- measurement

Question 15
- square roots
- integers

Zoe discovered a new island, which was named Island ABCDEF. She described the points of the island as follows:

- Point A is at (-4,4).
- Point B is 5 units to the right of Point A.
- The coordinates of Point C is $\frac{1}{4}$ of Point A's x- and y-coordinates.
- Point D is 15 km down from Point B.
- Point E is Point D reflected in the y-axis and then transformed 7.5 km to the left.
- The coordinates of Point F is twice that of Point C's x- and y-coordinates.

Plot the points on the grid and draw the island.

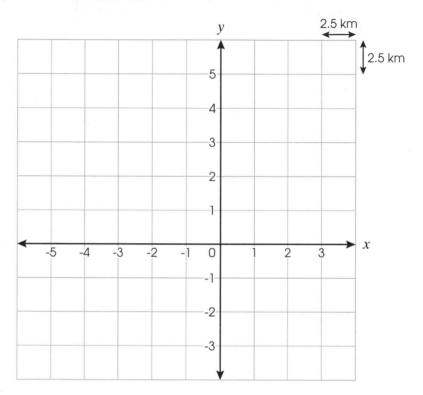

⑰ Refer to Question 16. What is the area of the island?

Topics covered:

Question 16
- fractions
- decimals
- Cartesian coordinate plane

Question 17
- measurement
- Cartesian coordinate plane

ISBN: 978-1-77149-205-8

⑱ Victoria is rolling a special dice that has 20 sides. She finds that the probability of rolling even numbers twice is 16%. How many even numbers are there on the dice?

⑲ Two lines cut a triangle as shown. What is the ratio of a to b to c?

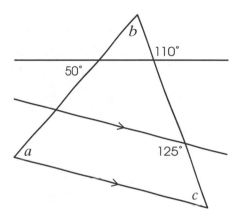

⑳ A stack of paper has a volume of 3013.2 cm³. Each sheet is $\frac{1}{10}$ mm thick. How many sheets of paper are there?

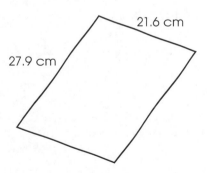

27.9 cm   21.6 cm

Topics covered:

Question 18	**Question 19**	**Question 20**
• square roots	• ratios	• fractions
• percents	• angles	• decimals
• algebra		• measurement
• probability		

Students are required to solve multi-step questions which involve various topics in each.

Topics Covered

	Number Sense and Numeration	Measurement	Geometry and Spatial Sense	Patterning and Algebra	Data Management and Probability	My Record ✔ correct ✗ incorrect
1	rates			algebra		
2	perfect squares square roots		angles			
3		measurement	Cartesian coordinate plane		probability	
4	ratios				data management	
5	percents ratios				data management	
6	percents			algebra		
7		measurement	angles			
8	multiples rates				data management	
9	factors	measurement				
10	integers fractions				probability	
11	perfect squares			algebra		
12	factors	measurement			probability	
13	rates			algebra		
14	fractions percents					
15			angles	algebra		
16	square roots rates	measurement				
17	fractions decimals/percents					
18	integers				data management	
19		measurement	Cartesian coordinate plane			
20		measurement	Cartesian coordinate plane		probability	

ISBN: 978-1-77149-205-8

① A car and a truck left a gas station in opposite directions. They were 214.5 km apart after 1.5 h. What were their average speeds if the car travelled 1.2 times as fast as the truck?

② What is the value of c if the values of a and b are 9^2 and $\sqrt{10000}$ respectively?

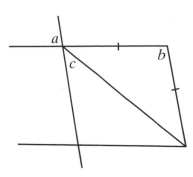

③ Simon is swimming somewhere on the grid shown. His x-coordinate is between -6 and 2 and his y-coordinate is between 1 and -4. Find the total possible area. What is the probability that he is in Quadrant III?

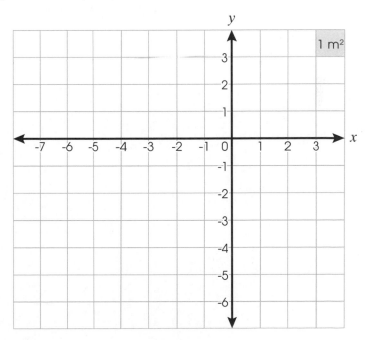

Topics covered:

Question 1
- rates
- algebra

Question 2
- perfect squares
- square roots
- angles

Question 3
- measurement
- Cartesian coordinate plane
- probability

ISBN: 978-1-77149-205-8

④ Robert recorded the number of rabbits and foxes in a forest each year. He created a double line graph to show the data. In which year was there a 2:1 ratio of rabbits to foxes?

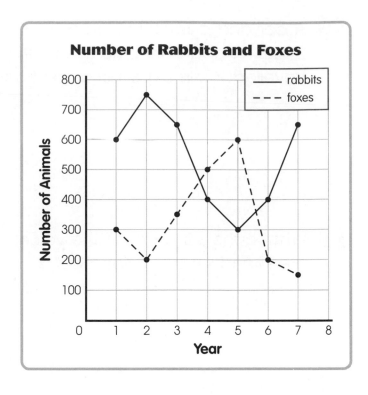

⑤ Refer to Question 4. In which year were 35% of all the animals foxes? What was the ratio of rabbits to foxes that year?

Topics covered:

Question 4
- ratios
- data management

Question 5
- percents
- ratios
- data management

ISBN: 978-1-77149-205-8

⑥ Melissa has $5, $10, and $20 bills. The numbers of $5 bills and $20 bills are the same and 40% of all her bills are $10 bills. If she has $345 in total, how many bills does she have?

⑦ Is Shape MNO a right triangle and Shape MOPR a trapezoid? If so, what is the area of Quadrilateral MNPR?

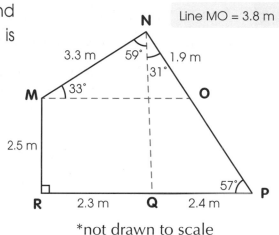

Line MO = 3.8 m

*not drawn to scale

⑧ Star stickers are sold in sheets of 15 for $3.20/sheet and heart stickers are sold in sheets of 18 for $4.80/sheet. If Carrie buys the same number of star and heart stickers, what is the mean cost of each sticker?

Topics covered:

Question 6
- percents
- algebra

Question 7
- measurement
- angles

Question 8
- multiples
- rates
- data management

ISBN: 978-1-77149-205-8

⑨ John had a block of Styrofoam that is 208 cm by 160 cm by 144 cm. He painted the surface area and then cut it into the largest possible identical cubes without any leftover Styrofoam. How many cubes are unpainted?

⑩ Wayne takes two fractions, $1\frac{3}{4}$ and $-\frac{3}{4}$, and performs one of the operations: addition, subtraction, multiplication, or division, with them. What is the probability that the answer is negative?

⑪ Jacob is thinking about a number. Half of the square of 8 is equal to that number times 4. What is the number?

Topics covered:

Question 9
- factors
- measurement

Question 10
- integers
- fractions
- probability

Question 11
- perfect squares
- algebra

ISBN: 978-1-77149-205-8

⑫ A rectangular field has an area of 30 m² where the length and width are both whole numbers. What is the probability that the perimeter of the field is less than 30 m?

⑬ Jackie drove 96 km to a conference. She drove for 54 min on the highway and 36 min on local roads. If she drove at a speed of 84 km/h on the highway, what was her speed on local roads?

⑭ Lucy made $4\frac{2}{5}$ L of soup. She gives 10% of it to her mom. How much more soup does Lucy have than her mom?

⑮ Neal has drawn a star design that contains a regular pentagon. The sum of all the angles in the regular pentagon is 540°. What is *b*?

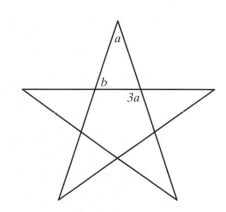

Topics covered:

Question 12	**Question 13**	**Question 14**	**Question 15**
• factors	• rates	• fractions	• angles
• measurement	• algebra	• percents	• algebra
• probability			

⑯ Kyle has a square backyard with an area of 64 m². He wants to fence 3 sides of the backyard which costs $64.50/m. How much does Kyle need to pay for fencing?

⑰ Andrea paid $10.92 for $\frac{3}{8}$ of a pizza, which included a 12% tax. What was the price of one whole pizza before tax?

⑱ Avery and Benny played a game with 5 rounds. In the end, Benny's mean score was 0.6 less than Avery's. What was Benny's median score?

Children's Scores

Round / Child	1	2	3	4	5
Avery	+3	-1	-2	+4	-5
Benny	-1	+2	-4	+6	?

Topics covered:

Question 16
- square roots
- rates
- measurement

Question 17
- fractions
- decimals
- percents

Question 18
- integers
- data management

ISBN: 978-1-77149-205-8

⑲ A tub has its corners at (-2,0), (0,-4), (4,0), and (0,2). What is the area of the tub?

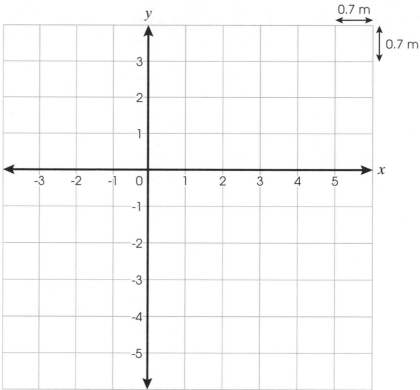

⑳ Refer to Question 19. Simon and Penny are both in the tub. What is the area of the tub that is in Quadrant IV? What is the probability that neither one of them are in Quadrant IV?

Topics covered:

Question 19
- measurement
- Cartesian coordinate plane

Question 20
- measurement
- Cartesian coordinate plane
- probability

ISBN: 978-1-77149-205-8

ISBN: 978-1-77149-205-8

■ Answers ··· ■

Basic Problem-solving Questions

1 Multiples and Factors

Math Skills

1.
```
      12
    3    4
   2      2
```
2 ; 2

2.
```
      18
    3    6
   2      3
```
2 × 3 × 3

3.
```
      24
    4      6
  2  2   2  3
```
2 × 2 × 2 × 3

4.
```
       28
    2     14
         2   7
```
2 × 2 × 7

5.
```
       36
    6      6
  2  3   2  3
```
2 × 2 × 3 × 3

6.
```
       40
    5      8
         2    4
             2   2
```
2 × 2 × 2 × 5

7. 6 ; 36
8. 12 ; 24
9. 6 ; 72
10. 12 ; 36
11. 6 ; 72
12. 4 ; 120
13. 2 ; 360

Problem Solving

```
    20
  2    10
      2   5
```
2 ; 2 ; 5
2 ; 5 ; 10
10

```
    30
  3    10
      2   5
```
2 ; 3 ; 5

1. No. of apples: 20 ÷ 10 = 2
   No. of oranges: 30 ÷ 10 = 3
   2 ; 3

2a. Balloons: 25 = 5 × 5
    Glow sticks: 35 = 5 × 7
    GCF of 25 and 35: 5
    5

 b. No. of balloons: 25 ÷ 5 = 5
    No. of glow sticks: 35 ÷ 5 = 7
    5 ; 7

 3. Tulips: 32 = 2 × 2 × 2 × 2 × 2
    Lilies: 40 = 2 × 2 × 2 × 5
    GCF of 32 and 40: 2 × 2 × 2 = 8
    No. of tulips: 32 ÷ 8 = 4
    No. of lilies: 40 ÷ 8 = 5
    4 ; 5

4. Baby carrots: 9 = 3 × 3
   Crackers: 12 = 2 × 2 × 3
   Grapes: 18 = 2 × 3 × 3
   GCF of 9, 12 ,and 18: 3
   No. of baby carrots: 9 ÷ 3 = 3
   No. of crackers: 12 ÷ 3 = 4
   No. of grapes: 18 ÷ 3 = 6
   3 ; 4 ; 6

5a. Boys: 39 = 3 × 13   Girls: 26 = 2 × 13
    GCF of 26 and 39: 13
    Groups of boys: 39 ÷ 13 = 3
    3

 b. Boys: 39 – 3 = 36 = 2 × 2 × 3 × 3
    Girls: 26 – 2 = 24 = 2 × 2 × 2 × 3
    GCF of 24 and 36: 2 × 2 × 3 = 12
    Groups of girls: 24 ÷ 12 = 2
    12 ; 2

6a. Patties: 8 = 2 × 2 × 2
    Buns: 12 = 2 × 2 × 3
    LCM of 8 and 12: 2 × 2 × 2 × 3 = 24
    Harvey will make at least 24 burgers.

 b. Packages of patties: 24 ÷ 8 = 3
    Packages of buns: 24 ÷ 12 = 2
    Harvey will buy 3 packages of patties and
    2 packages of buns.

7. Eastbound bus: 6 = 2 × 3
   Westbound bus: 8 = 2 × 2 × 2
   LCM of 6 and 8: 2 × 2 × 2 × 3 = 24
   It will be after 24 minutes.

8. Lamppost: 11 = 1 × 11
   Tree: 7 = 1 × 7
   LCM of 7 and 11: 7 × 11 = 77
   It will be 77 m.

9a. Manual: 30 = 2 × 3 × 5
    Novel: 40 = 2 × 2 × 2 × 5
    LCM of 30 and 40: 2 × 2 × 2 × 3 × 5 = 120
    At least 120 sheets were used.

 b. Copies of manual: 120 ÷ 30 = 4
    Copies of novel: 120 ÷ 40 = 3
    There were 4 manuals and 3 novels.

10a. Children: 12 = 2 × 2 × 3
     Adults: 26 = 2 × 13
     LCM of 12 and 26: 2 × 2 × 3 × 13 = 156
     Total fee: $156 + $156 = $312
     The group paid at least $312 in all.

  b. No. of children: $156 ÷ $12 = 13
     No. of adults: $156 ÷ $26 = 6
     There were 13 children and 6 adults.

11. 5 = 1 × 5   9 = 3 × 3
    15 = 3 × 5
    LCM of 5, 9, and 15: 3 × 3 × 5 = 45
    Multiples of 45: 45, 90, ~~135~~ ← over 100
    Tom could have 45 or 90 postcards.

ISBN: 978-1-77149-205-8

12. Bacon: $96 = 2 \times 2 \times 2 \times 2 \times 2 \times 3$
Lettuce: $72 = 2 \times 2 \times 2 \times 3 \times 3$
Tomato: $48 = 2 \times 2 \times 2 \times 2 \times 3$
GCF of 48, 72, and 96: $2 \times 2 \times 2 \times 3 = 24$
Pieces of bacon: $96 \div 24 = 4$
Leaves of lettuce: $72 \div 24 = 3$
Slices of tomato: $48 \div 24 = 2$
She can make 24 sandwiches at most.
Each sandwich will have 4 pieces of bacon, 3 leaves of lettuce, and 2 slices of tomato.

13. Teacup ride: $15 = 3 \times 5$
Carousel: $18 = 2 \times 3 \times 3$
LCM of 15 and 18: $2 \times 3 \times 3 \times 5 = 90$
No. of times teacup ride ran: $90 \div 15 = 6$
No. of times carousel ran: $90 \div 18 = 5$
The teacup ride ran at least 6 times. The carousel ran at least 5 times.

14. Jupiter: $12 = 2 \times 2 \times 3$
Saturn: $30 = 2 \times 3 \times 5$
Uranus: $84 = 2 \times 2 \times 3 \times 7$
LCM of 12, 30, and 84: $2 \times 2 \times 3 \times 5 \times 7 = 420$
Next alignment: $1926 + 420 = 2346$
The planets will align again in 2346.

15. Train A: $18 = 2 \times 3 \times 3$
Train B: $27 = 3 \times 3 \times 3$
LCM of 18 and 27: $2 \times 3 \times 3 \times 3 = 54$
Previous time: 6:45 p.m. – 54 min = 5:51 p.m.
The trains last arrived together at 5:51 p.m.

16a. Red beads: $64 = 2 \times 2 \times 2 \times 2 \times 2 \times 2$
Blue beads: $80 = 2 \times 2 \times 2 \times 2 \times 5$
GCF of 64 and 80: $2 \times 2 \times 2 \times 2 = 16$
Miriam can make 16 bracelets at most.

b. No. of red beads: $64 \div 16 = 4$
No. of blue beads: $80 \div 16 = 5$
There will be 4 red and 5 blue beads.

c. LCM of 64 and 80:
$2 \times 2 \times 2 \times 2 \times 2 \times 2 \times 5 = 320$
Miriam will have at least 320 beads of each colour.

17a. Box A: $30 = 2 \times 3 \times 5$
Box B: $45 = 3 \times 3 \times 5$
LCM of 30 and 45: $2 \times 3 \times 3 \times 5 = 90$
Each shelf is at least 90 cm tall.

b. GCF of 30 and 45: $3 \times 5 = 15$
The maximum height is 15 cm.

2　Perfect Squares and Square Roots

Math Skills

1. 16 ; 64 ; 49 ; 9 ; 25
2a. 1 ; 4 ; 9 ; 16 ; 25 ; 36 ; 49 ; 64 ; 81 ; 100 ; 121 ; 144 ; 169 ; 196 ; 225 ; 256 ; 289 ; 324 ; 361 ; 400

b. 1 ; 2 ; 3 ; 4 ; 5 ; 6 ; 7 ; 8 ; 9 ; 10 ; 11 ; 12 ; 13 ; 14 ; 15 ; 16 ; 17 ; 18 ; 19 ; 20

Problem Solving

256 ; 17 ; $\sqrt{289}$; 150 ; 16^2 ; Wesley

1. $12^2 = 12 \times 12 = 144$
144

2. $19^2 = 19 \times 19 = 361$
361

3. $36^2 = 36 \times 36 = 1296$; 1296

4. Square rug: $2^2 = 2 \times 2 = 4$ ← greater than 3.5
square rug

5a. $30^2 = 30 \times 30 = 900$
900

b. $6^2 = 6 \times 6 = 36$
36

c. Side length of each cookie: $30 \div 6 = 5$
Area of each cookie: $5^2 = 5 \times 5 = 25$
25

6a. $5^2 = 5 \times 5 = 25$
The area of the square tiles is 25 cm².

b. No. of tiles: $25^2 = 25 \times 25 = 625$
Area of the design: $25 \times 625 = 15\,625$
The area of the design is 15 625 cm².

7a. $12^2 = 12 \times 12 = 144$
There are 144 tiles in total.

b. Area of each tile: $2^2 = 2 \times 2 = 4$
Area of the board: $4 \times 144 = 576$
The area of the board is 576 cm².

8. $\sqrt{324} = 18$
The side length of Murray's farm is 18 m.

9. $\sqrt{484} = 22$
There will be 22 rows.

10. Largest quilt possible:
$22^2 = 22 \times 22 = 484$
$23^2 = 23 \times 23 = 529$ ← greater than 500
Remaining pieces: $500 - 484 = 16$
16 pieces will be left.

11. $18^2 = 18 \times 18 = 324$ ← greater than 320
Yes, the painting will fit.

12. Greatest possible area:
$31^2 = 31 \times 31 = 961$
$32^2 = 32 \times 32 = 1024$ ← greater than 1000
There will be 31 tiles in each row.

13. $\sqrt{729} = 27$　　　$\sqrt{961} = 31$
Difference: $31 - 27 = 4$
The difference is 4 cm.

14a. $15^2 = 15 \times 15 = 225$
The area of the tile is 225 cm².

b. $\sqrt{9} = 3$ (m) = 300 (cm)
No. of tiles in each row: $300 \div 15 = 20$
20 tiles are needed for each row.

c. Circles in each tile: $5^2 = 5 \times 5 = 25$
No. of tiles in design: $20^2 = 20 \times 20 = 400$
No. of circles in design: $25 \times 400 = 10\,000$
The flooring design has 10 000 circles.

ISBN: 978-1-77149-205-8

15a. $\sqrt{576} = 24$
The side length of the collage is 24 cm.
b. Side length of each photo: $24 \div 3 = 8$
Perimeter of each photo: $8 \times 4 = 32$
The perimeter of each square photo is 32 cm.
16a. Side length of cloth: $\sqrt{121} = 11$
Perimeter of cloth: $11 \times 4 = 44$
Perimeter of towel: $44 \times 4 = 176$
The perimeter of the towel is 176 cm.
b. $44^2 = 44 \times 44 = 1936$
The area of the towel is 1936 cm².
17. Blocks in each layer: $5^2 = 5 \times 5 = 25$
Total blocks: $25 \times 25 = 625$
Catherine used 625 blocks.

3 Integers

Math Skills

1a. 2
b. -5
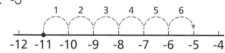
c. -13
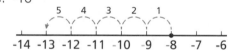
2. -6   3. -17   4. 1
5. 20   6. 28   7. -9
8. -3   9. -35   10. 54
11. -2   12. -9   13. 8
14. 2 ; 5   15. -24 ; -8   16. 20 ; 28
17. $(-4) - 9$; -13   18. $-16 \times (-3)$; 48
19. $91 + (-9)$; 82   20. $(-32) \div (-4)$; 8
21. $30 \div (-15)$; -2   22. $4 \times (-3)$; -12

Problem Solving

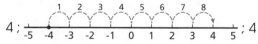
4 ; ; 4

1a. $(-16) - 12 = -28$ b. $(-10) - (-16) = 6$
-28   6
2a. $8 - (-6) = 14$; 14
b. Nancy: Conrad:
$(-6) + 9 = 3$; 3 $8 + (-11) = -3$; -3
c. $3 - (-3) = 6$
Yes, Nancy had a higher total score by 6 points.
3a. $(-35) + 27 = -8$ b. $50 - (-8) = 58$
-8   58
4a. $11 - (-3) = 14$ b. $(-3) - (-15) = 12$
14   12
5a. $1 - (-5) = 6$
The time difference is 6 hours.

b. $(-5) - (-13) = 8$
The time difference is 8 hours.
6a. $(-4) \times 5 = -20$
The total change of the shares was -$20.
b. Change of 1 share: $(-4) + (-8) = -12$
Change of 5 shares: $(-12) \times 5 = -60$
The total change of the shares is -$60.
7a. $(-25) \times 5 = -125$
The expected total change was -$125.
b. $(-35) \div 5 = -7$
The average change each day was -$7.
8. $(-18) \div 6 = -3$
The change for each floor was -3 m.
9. $(-13) \times 3 = -39$
The total change in value was -$39.
10a. Kingston and Ottawa: $4 - (-2) = 6$
The difference is 6°C.
Toronto and Sudbury: $(-4) - (-14) = 10$
The difference is 10°C.
Ottawa and Sudbury: $(-2) - (-14) = 12$
The difference is 12°C.
b. $((-14) + (-4) + 4 + (-2)) \div 4 = (-16) \div 4 = -4$
The average temperature is -4°C.
c. $((-6) \times 2 + (-5) + (-1) \times 4) \div 7 = (-21) \div 7 = -3$
The average temperature will be -3°C.
11a. Andrew: $3 \times 3 + (-2) \times 5 = 9 + (-10) = -1$
Andrew had a score of -1.
Zack: $3 \times 2 + (-2) \times 3 = 6 + (-6) = 0$
Zack had a score of 0.
Ryan: $3 \times 4 + (-2) \times 2 = 12 + (-4) = 8$
Ryan had a score of 8.
b. $8 > 0 > -1$
1st place: Ryan   3rd place: Andrew
Difference: $8 - (-1) = 9$
Ryan won the contest. He got 9 more points.
c. $9 \div 3 = 3$
Andrew should have answered 3 more questions correctly.

4 Fractions

Math Skills

1. $= \dfrac{8}{10} + \dfrac{7}{10} = \dfrac{15}{10} = 1\dfrac{5}{10} = 1\dfrac{1}{2}$

2. $= \dfrac{11}{12} - \dfrac{4}{12} = \dfrac{7}{12}$

3. $= \dfrac{\cancel{5} \times \cancel{4}^{1}}{\cancel{8} \times \cancel{15}_{3}} = \dfrac{1}{6}$

4. $= \dfrac{2}{3} \times \dfrac{9}{2} = \dfrac{\cancel{2} \times \cancel{9}^{3}}{\cancel{3} \times \cancel{2}_{1}} = 3$

5. $1\dfrac{11}{15}$ 6. $4\dfrac{1}{24}$ 7. $4\dfrac{11}{12}$

ISBN: 978-1-77149-205-8

8. $3\frac{10}{21}$

9. $\frac{13}{14}$

10. $\frac{8}{9}$

11. $1\frac{1}{3}$

12. $\frac{1}{12}$

13. $\frac{1}{6}$

14. $\frac{63}{64}$

15. $2\frac{2}{3}$

16. 9

17. $\frac{4}{7}$

18. $2\frac{1}{4}$

19. 6

20. $10\frac{4}{5}$

21. $= \frac{\overset{3}{\cancel{9}}}{\underset{1}{\cancel{4}}} \times \frac{\overset{2}{\cancel{8}}}{\underset{1}{\cancel{3}}} - 4\frac{1}{5} = 6 - 4\frac{1}{5} = 1\frac{4}{5}$

22. $= \frac{\overset{3}{\cancel{27}}}{\underset{4}{\cancel{20}}} \times \frac{\overset{1}{\cancel{5}}}{\underset{1}{\cancel{9}}} + 2\frac{5}{8} = \frac{3}{4} + 2\frac{5}{8} = \frac{6}{8} + 2\frac{5}{8} = 3\frac{3}{8}$

23. $= (\frac{42}{15} - \frac{35}{15}) \times 3\frac{3}{14} = \frac{\overset{1}{\cancel{7}}}{\underset{1}{\cancel{15}}} \times \frac{\overset{3}{\cancel{45}}}{\underset{2}{\cancel{14}}} = \frac{3}{2} = 1\frac{1}{2}$

24. $= 8\frac{1}{2} \div (\frac{25}{10} + \frac{26}{10}) = 8\frac{1}{2} \div \frac{51}{10} = \frac{\overset{1}{\cancel{17}}}{\underset{1}{\cancel{2}}} \times \frac{\overset{5}{\cancel{10}}}{\underset{3}{\cancel{51}}}$

$= \frac{5}{3} = 1\frac{2}{3}$

Problem Solving

$3\frac{17}{20}$; $2\frac{5}{20}$; $1\frac{12}{20}$; $3\frac{17}{20}$; $3\frac{17}{20}$

1. $1\frac{5}{7} + \frac{13}{14} = 1\frac{10}{14} + \frac{13}{14} = 1\frac{23}{14} = 2\frac{9}{14}$; $2\frac{9}{14}$

2. $2\frac{1}{2} + 1\frac{4}{5} + \frac{3}{4} = 2\frac{10}{20} + 1\frac{16}{20} + \frac{15}{20} = 3\frac{41}{20}$

$= 5\frac{1}{20}$; $5\frac{1}{20}$

3a. $3\frac{2}{3} + 4\frac{5}{6} = 3\frac{4}{6} + 4\frac{5}{6} = 7\frac{9}{6} = 8\frac{1}{2}$; $8\frac{1}{2}$

b. $8\frac{1}{2} - 2\frac{5}{12} = 8\frac{6}{12} - 2\frac{5}{12} = 6\frac{1}{12}$; $6\frac{1}{12}$

4a. $4\frac{5}{6} + 1\frac{2}{5} = 4\frac{25}{30} + 1\frac{12}{30} = 5\frac{37}{30} = 6\frac{7}{30}$; $6\frac{7}{30}$

b. Jess: $6\frac{7}{30} - \frac{4}{3} = 4\frac{67}{30} - \frac{40}{30} = 4\frac{27}{30} = 4\frac{9}{10}$

Difference:

$4\frac{9}{10} - 4\frac{5}{6} = 4\frac{27}{30} - 4\frac{25}{30} = \frac{2}{30} = \frac{1}{15}$; $\frac{1}{15}$

5. $10 - 4\frac{1}{6} - 3\frac{4}{9} = 9\frac{18}{18} - 4\frac{3}{18} - 3\frac{8}{18} = 2\frac{7}{18}$

$2\frac{7}{18}$

6. $\frac{1}{6} \times 12 = \frac{1}{\cancel{6}} \times \frac{\overset{2}{\cancel{12}}}{1} = 2$

Mrs. Grand used 2 cans of tomato sauce.

7. $\frac{1}{7} \times 5\frac{1}{4} = \frac{1}{\cancel{7}} \times \frac{\overset{3}{\cancel{21}}}{4} = \frac{3}{4}$

$\frac{3}{4}$ of the pot will be filled.

8a. $2\frac{1}{3} \times 3\frac{1}{2} = \frac{7}{3} \times \frac{7}{2} = \frac{49}{6} = 8\frac{1}{6}$

$8\frac{1}{6}$ cups of sugar are needed.

b. $24 \times 3\frac{1}{2} = \frac{\overset{12}{\cancel{24}}}{1} \times \frac{7}{\underset{1}{\cancel{2}}} = 84$

84 cookies will be made.

9a. $18\frac{3}{4} \div \frac{3}{4} = \frac{\overset{25}{\cancel{75}}}{\underset{1}{\cancel{4}}} \times \frac{\overset{1}{\cancel{4}}}{\underset{1}{\cancel{3}}} = 25$

There are 25 episodes in the series.

b. $60 \times \frac{3}{4} = \frac{\overset{15}{\cancel{60}}}{1} \times \frac{3}{\underset{1}{\cancel{4}}} = 45$

Each episode is 45 minutes long.

10a. $5\frac{5}{9} \times 3\frac{3}{5} = \frac{\overset{10}{\cancel{50}}}{\underset{1}{\cancel{9}}} \times \frac{\overset{2}{\cancel{18}}}{\underset{1}{\cancel{5}}} = 20$

The carousel will make 20 revolutions.

b. $15 \div 5\frac{5}{9} = \frac{\overset{3}{\cancel{15}}}{1} \times \frac{9}{\underset{10}{\cancel{50}}} = \frac{27}{10} = 2\frac{7}{10}$

It will take $2\frac{7}{10}$ minutes.

11. $33 \div \frac{1}{4} = \frac{33}{1} \times \frac{4}{1} = 132$

There were 132 pieces of chocolate.

12. $1\frac{3}{4} \div 2\frac{1}{3} \times \frac{5}{6} = \frac{\overset{1}{\cancel{7}}}{4} \times \frac{\overset{1}{\cancel{3}}}{\underset{1}{\cancel{7}}} \times \frac{5}{\underset{2}{\cancel{6}}} = \frac{5}{8}$

Jonathan can swim $\frac{5}{8}$ laps in $\frac{5}{6}$ min.

13. $(4 - 1\frac{2}{3}) \div \frac{2}{5} = (3\frac{3}{3} - 1\frac{2}{3}) \div \frac{2}{5} = 2\frac{1}{3} \div \frac{2}{5}$

$= \frac{7}{3} \times \frac{5}{2} = \frac{35}{6} = 5\frac{5}{6}$

The capacity of the container is $5\frac{5}{6}$ L.

14a. Total hours:

$3\frac{2}{3} + 2\frac{5}{6} + 3\frac{1}{5} = 3\frac{20}{30} + 2\frac{25}{30} + 3\frac{6}{30} = 8\frac{51}{30}$

$= 9\frac{21}{30} = 9\frac{7}{10}$

Average: $9\frac{7}{10} \div 3 = \frac{97}{10} \times \frac{1}{3} = \frac{97}{30} = 3\frac{7}{30}$

On average, Mr. Smith spent $3\frac{7}{30}$ hours working on his experiment each day.

b. Remaining experiment: $1 - \frac{3}{5} = \frac{2}{5}$

Time:

$9\frac{7}{10} \div \frac{3}{5} \times \frac{2}{5} = \frac{97}{\underset{5}{\cancel{10}}} \times \frac{\overset{1}{\cancel{5}}}{3} \times \frac{\overset{1}{\cancel{2}}}{5} = \frac{97}{15} = 6\frac{7}{15}$

Mr. Smith needs $6\frac{7}{15}$ more hours.

15. $32\frac{1}{8} + \frac{5}{6} \times 9 = 32\frac{1}{8} + \frac{5}{\underset{2}{\cancel{6}}} \times \frac{\overset{3}{\cancel{9}}}{1} = 32\frac{1}{8} + \frac{15}{2}$

$= 32\frac{1}{8} + 7\frac{1}{2} = 32\frac{1}{8} + 7\frac{4}{8} = 39\frac{5}{8}$

Tony's plant will be $39\frac{5}{8}$ cm tall.

16a. Martin:

$7\frac{1}{2} \div 1\frac{1}{3} = \frac{15}{2} \times \frac{3}{4} = \frac{45}{8} = 5\frac{5}{8}$

Bryan:

$5\frac{5}{12} \div \frac{5}{6} = \frac{\overset{13}{\cancel{65}}}{\underset{2}{\cancel{12}}} \times \frac{\overset{1}{\cancel{6}}}{\underset{1}{\cancel{5}}} = \frac{13}{2} = 6\frac{1}{2}$

ISBN: 978-1-77149-205-8

Difference:

$$6\frac{1}{2} - 5\frac{5}{8} = 5\frac{12}{8} - 5\frac{5}{8} = \frac{7}{8}$$

Bryan drinks $\frac{7}{8}$ cup more in a day.

b. $20 \div 5\frac{5}{8} = 20 \div \frac{45}{8} = \frac{\cancel{20}^{4}}{1} \times \frac{8}{\cancel{45}_{9}} = \frac{32}{9} = 3\frac{5}{9}$

It will take Martin $3\frac{5}{9}$ days.

17a. Girls: $1 - \frac{9}{20} = \frac{11}{20}$

No. of students: $33 \div \frac{11}{20} = \frac{\cancel{33}^{3}}{1} \times \frac{20}{\cancel{11}_{1}} = 60$

There are 60 students in total.

b. No. of grade 7 students:

$60 \times \frac{7}{15} = \frac{\cancel{60}^{4}}{1} \times \frac{7}{\cancel{15}_{1}} = 28$

No. of grade 7 girls: $28 - 15 = 13$

Fraction of girls in grade 7: $\frac{13}{33}$

$\frac{13}{33}$ of the girls are in grade 7.

5 Decimals

Math Skills

1. 44.12

2. 7.24

3.
```
      7.7
  ×   4.3
      231
     3080
    33.11
```

4.
```
      5.2
  4)20.8
     20
      8
      8
```

5. 17.53
6. 26.263
7. 19.2

8. 35.09
9. 6.881
10. 11.367

11. 2.34
12. 8.42
13. 0.63

14. 2.253
15. 2.195
16. 7.182

17. 10.912
18. 10.2204
19. 13.398

20. 133.848
21. 18.5136
22. 10.2442

23. 8.46
24. 0.15
25. 66

26. 22.6
27. 20.6
28. 3.01

29. $= 1.54 \div 1.1$
$= 1.4$

30. $= 1.65 \times 2.482$
$= 4.0953$

31. $= 8.722 + 8$
$= 16.722$

32. $= 3.88 \times 2.5$
$= 9.7$

Problem Solving

256.33 ; 256.33 ; 256.33

1a. $256.33 + 14.608 = 270.938$; 270.938

b. $270.938 - 130.43 = 140.508$; 140.508

2a. $\$34.99 + \$19.95 = \$54.94$; 54.94

b. $\$54.94 + \$7.14 = \$62.08$; 62.08

3. $\$150 - \$97.62 = \$52.38$; 52.38

4. $9.07 - 1.238 = 7.832$; 7.832

5a. $16.273 - 9.109 = 7.164$; 7.164

b. $25 - 16.273 = 8.727$; 8.727

6a. $\$20 \times 1.26 = \$25.20$

Kylie would need $25.20 yesterday.

b. $\$20 \times 1.305 = \$26.10$

Kylie would need $26.10 today.

7a. $200 \times 4.219 = 843.8$

The actual distance is 843.8 m.

b. $200 \times 2.301 = 460.2$

Trail A is actually 460.2 m longer.

8. $\$2.12 \div \$0.025 = 84.8$

84.8 megabytes are used.

9. $\$45.51 \div \$1.025 = 44.4$

Lina filled 44.4 L of gas.

10a. $\$44.16 \div 345 = \$0.128$

1 kWh of electricity cost $0.128 on average.

b. $(\$44.16 - \$35.07) \div 0.18$
$= \$9.09 \div 0.18$
$= 50.5$

50.5 on-peak hours were charged.

11a. $(2.6 + 4.825 + 0.855) \times 2$
$= 8.28 \times 2$
$= 16.56$

There will be 16.56 L of fruit punch.

b. $8.28 \div 16 = 0.5175$ (L) $= 517.5$ (mL)

There is 517.5 mL of fruit punch in 1 cup.

12a. $\$21.35 \times 2.4 = \$51.24$

There will be $51.24 in Marsha's savings.

b. $(\$51.24 - \$22.39) \times 0.55$
$= \$28.85 \times 0.55$
$= \$15.8675$

The gift will be $15.87.

13. $(2.408 \div 0.05) - 2.408$
$= 48.16 - 2.408$
$= 45.752$

Conner weighed 45.752 kg before.

14a. $\$15.99 \times 3 + \$32.65 \times 2$
$= \$47.97 + \$65.30$
$= \$113.27$

They cost $113.27.

b. $\$26.65 \times 2 - (\$15.99 + \$32.65)$
$= \$53.30 - \$48.64$
$= \$4.66$

2 sweaters cost $4.66 more.

c. $\$15.99 \times 5 \div \$26.65$
$= \$79.95 \div \$26.65$
$= 3$

3 sweaters can be bought.

15. $(\$20.57 - \$8.79) \div \$14.725$
$= \$11.78 \div \$14.725$
$= 0.8$

Janice used 0.8 L of gasoline.

16. $\$17.45 \times 1.202 - \$15.25 \times 0.824$
$= \$20.9749 - \$12.566$
$= \$8.4089$

The pork costs $8.41 more than the beef.

6 Percents

Math Skills

1a. $\dfrac{1}{5}$

b. $\dfrac{32}{100}$; $\dfrac{8}{25}$

c. $\dfrac{10}{100}$; $\dfrac{1}{10}$

d. $\dfrac{6}{100}$; $\dfrac{3}{50}$

e. $\dfrac{84}{100}$; $\dfrac{21}{25}$

f. $\dfrac{105}{100}$; $1\dfrac{1}{20}$

2. 15 ; 30

3. $= 64 \times 25\%$
$= 64 \times \dfrac{25}{100}$
$= 16$

4. $= 2 \times 50\%$
$= 2 \times \dfrac{50}{100}$
$= 1$

5. $= 300 \times 1\%$
$= 300 \times \dfrac{1}{100}$
$= 3$

6. $= 50 \times 8\%$
$= 50 \times \dfrac{8}{100}$
$= 4$

7. $= 95 \times 120\%$
$= 95 \times \dfrac{120}{100}$
$= 114$

8a. 0.27 b. 0.43 c. 0.05
d. 0.18 e. 1.12 f. 0.03
g. 0.94

9. 0.1 ; 9

10. $= 44 \times 75\%$
$= 44 \times 0.75$
$= 33$

11. $= 150 \times 6\%$
$= 150 \times 0.06$
$= 9$

12. $= 12 \times 50\%$
$= 12 \times 0.5$
$= 6$

13. $= 200 \times 48\%$
$= 200 \times 0.48$
$= 96$

14. $= 10 \times 105\%$
$= 10 \times 1.05$
$= 10.5$

Problem Solving

0.2 ; 5 ; 5 ; 20 ; 20

1. Discount:
$\$190.50 \times 15\% = \$190.50 \times 0.15 = \$28.575$
Sale price: $\$190.50 - \$28.575 = \$161.925$
161.93

2a. Tax: $\$125 \times 5\% = \$125 \times 0.05 = \$6.25$
Total cost: $\$125 + \$6.25 = \$131.25$
131.25

b. Tax: $\$125 \times 13\% = \$125 \times 0.13 = \$16.25$
Total cost: $\$125 + \$16.25 = \$141.25$
141.25

c. Tax: $\$125 \times 12\% = \$125 \times 0.12 = \$15$
Total cost: $\$125 + \$15 = \$140$
140

3. Discount: $\$180 \times 15\% = \$180 \times 0.15 = \$27$
Sale price: $\$180 - \$27 = \$153$
Tax: $\$153 \times 14\% = \$153 \times 0.14 = \$21.42$
Total cost: $\$153 + \$21.42 = \$174.42$
174.42

4. Percent of yellow apple trees:
$100\% - 80\% - 15\% = 5\%$
No. of yellow apple trees:
$260 \times 5\% = 260 \times 0.05 = 13$
13

5. Percent of girls: $100\% - 25\% = 75\%$
No. of girls: $56 \times 75\% = 56 \times 0.75 = 42$
42

6. Percent with computers:
$100\% - 35\% - 20\% = 45\%$
Users with computers:
$180 \times 45\% = 180 \times 0.45 = 81$
81

7. Bleach: $1050 \times 5\% = 1050 \times 0.05 = 52.5$
Water: $1050 - 52.5 = 997.5$
997.5

8. Ribbon used: $5 \times 30\% = 5 \times 0.3 = 1.5$
Ribbon remaining: $5 - 1.5 = 3.5$
3.5 m of ribbon remains.

9. Paint spilled: $3.85 \times 8\% = 3.85 \times 0.08 = 0.308$
Paint remaining: $3.85 - 0.308 = 3.542$
3.542 L of paint is still in the can.

10a. Discount amount: $\$61 - \$45.75 = \$15.25$
Discount in percent: $\$15.25 \div \$61 = 25\%$
The discount is 25%.

b. Discount:
$\$27.50 \times 25\% = \$27.50 \times 0.25 = \$6.875$
Sale price: $\$27.50 - \$6.875 = \$20.625$
The belt is $20.63.

11a. Total books: $204 + 51 + 45 = 300$
Percent of novels: $204 \div 300 = 0.68 = 68\%$
68% of the books are novels.

b. Not magazines: $300 - 45 = 255$
Percent of books that are not magazines:
$255 \div 300 = 0.85 = 85\%$
85% of the books are not magazines.

12. Total butter: $45.2 + 67.8 = 113$
Percent remaining: $67.8 \div 113 = 0.6 = 60\%$
60% of the stick of butter remains.

13. Cost: $\$17.95 + \$15.55 = \$33.50$
Tax: $\$38.19 - \$33.50 = \$4.69$
Tax rate: $\$4.69 \div \$33.50 = 0.14 = 14\%$
The tax rate was 14%.

14a. $12 \div 40 = 0.3 = 30\%$
30% of the people have flowers only.

b. People with trees: $14 + 2 = 16$
Percent with trees: $16 \div 40 = 0.4 = 40\%$
40% of the people have trees.

15a. Area of wall: $3 \times 5 = 15$
Percent painted: $3 \div 15 = 0.2 = 20\%$
20% of the wall is painted.

b. $100\% - 20\% = 80\%$
80% of the wall is not painted.

ISBN: 978-1-77149-205-8

16. Interest in 1 year:
$1980 × 4% = $1980 × 0.04 = $79.20
Interest in 6 years: $79.20 × 6 = $475.20
Total: $1980 + $475.20 = $2455.20
Margaret will have $2455.20 in total.

17a. 10 ÷ 250 = 0.04 = 4%
4% of the lemonade is syrup.
b. 1 L = 1000 mL
1000 × 4% = 1000 × 0.04 = 40
There was 40 mL of syrup in the pitcher.

18a. 35 × 40% = 35 × 0.4 = 14
There are 14 nickels.
b. No. of dimes: 35 – 14 = 21
Total from dimes: $0.10 × 21 = $2.10
Total from nickels: $0.05 × 14 = $0.70
Total: $2.10 + $0.70 = $2.80
Percent from nickels:
$0.70 ÷ $2.80 = 0.25 = 25%
25% of the money amount is nickels.

19. Percent harvested: 100% – 82% = 18%
Total tomatoes:
450 ÷ 18% = 450 ÷ 0.18 = 2500
Remaining tomatoes: 2500 – 450 = 2050
2050 tomatoes remain.

7 Ratios and Rates

Math Skills

1a. 8:4 ; 4:8 ; 4:12   b. 4:2 ; 3:1 ; 2:5 ; 1:9
2. 9:15 ; 15:25   3:4 ; 18:24
    4:2 ; 16:8   6:9 ; 8:12
    10:12 ; 25:30   5:2 ; 25:10
3a. 2.55   b. 0.25   c. 0.33
d. 32   e. 78   f. 82.5
g. 68

Problem Solving

15 ; 8 ; 15 ; 8 ; 45 ; 45

1a. red to blue = 2:3 = 6:9
6
b. red to total = 2:5 = 12:30   (2+3)
12
2a. boys to girls = 3:2 = 27:18
Difference: 27 – 18 = 9
9
b. girls to all = 2:5 = 12:30   (2+3)
12
3a. roses to tulips = 3:4 = 15:20
Difference: 20 – 15 = 5
5
b. roses to tulips = 3:4 = 18:24
Remaining tulips: 24 – 20 = 4
4

4a. red to blue = 2:3 = 4:6
Purple paint: 4 + 6 = 10
10
b. red to blue to purple = 2:3:5 = 6:9:15   (2+3)
6 ; 9
5a. vinegar to dressing = 5:8 = 30:48
30
b. vinegar to dressing = 5:6 = 40:48   (5+1)
40
6a. 352 ÷ 8 = 44
Rhonda's typing speed is 44 words/min.
b. 44 × 30 = 1320
Rhonda can type 1320 words.
7. ValueMart: $1.50 ÷ 3 apples = $0.50/apple
FruitShop: $2.35 ÷ 5 apples = $0.47/apple
FruitShop is the better buy.
8. Package of 6: $2.10 ÷ 6 rolls = $0.35/roll
Package of 20: $6.80 ÷ 20 rolls = $0.34/roll
Savings: 0.35 – 0.34 = 0.01
Rosie will save $0.01/roll.
9. Speed: 756 ÷ 5 = 151.2
Distance: 151.2 × 8.5 = 1285.2
The plane can travel 1285.2 km.
10. Rate: 162 ÷ 15 = 10.8
Distance: 10.8 × 75 = 810
Lowell can drive 810 km.
11. Cost: $6.84 ÷ 12 muffins = $0.57/muffin
New cost: 0.57 + 0.07 = 0.64
Cost of 10 muffins: 0.64 × 10 = 6.4
10 muffins cost $6.40 now.
12. Speed: 3 ÷ 0.25 = 12
Distance: 12 × 1.5 = 18
Time needed: 18 ÷ 50 = 0.36
It will take the car 0.36 h.
13a. red to all = 5:11 = 100:220   (5+6)
The mass of the red beads is 100 g.
b. Rate: $2 ÷ 80 g = $0.025/g
Cost: 0.025 × 220 = 5.5
The rate is $0.025/g. The cost of buying
the beads is $5.50.
c. Total mass: 7.7 ÷ 0.025 = 308
red to all = 5:11 = 140:308
140 g of red beads were bought.
14a. Car rate: $128.85 ÷ 3 days = $42.95/day
Difference: (96.55 – 42.95) × 5 = 268
It will cost $268 more to rent a van.
b. 96.55 × 5 = 482.75 < 600
Yes, Maria is able to rent a van.
15a. vanilla to chocolate = 2:1 = 10:5
vanilla to strawberry = 5:3 = 10:6
vanilla to chocolate to strawberry
× 100
= 10:5:6 = 1000:500:600
600 g of strawberry ice cream is needed.

ISBN: 978-1-77149-205-8

b. vanilla to chocolate to strawberry to all

$= 10{:}5{:}6{:}21 \xrightarrow{\times 0.08} = 0.8{:}0.4{:}0.48{:}1.68$
(10+5+6)

The weights of vanilla, chocolate, and strawberry ice cream are 0.8 kg, 0.4 kg, and 0.48 kg respectively.

16a. reading to playing sports = 2:3 = 90:135
90 min = 1.5 h
Peter spent 1.5 h on reading.

b. $33 \div 1.5 = 22$
Peter's rate was 22 pages/h.

17. Before raise: Sammy:Davis = 3:4 = 9:12
Davis's pay was $12/h.
After raise: Sammy:Davis = 4:3 = 16:12
Sammy's pay is now $16/h.
Sammy's earnings: $16 \times 40 = 640$
Sammy will earn $640.

8 Measurement

Math Skills

A: 10.4 cm ; 5.632 cm²
B: 19.7 m ; 17.36 m²
C: 24.1 cm ; 35.75 cm²
D: 31.6 m ; 34 m²
E: 8.5 cm ; 2 cm²
F: 508.4 cm² ; 668.856 cm³
G: 142.64 m² ; 97.44 m³
H: 128.28 m² ; 83.16 m³
I: 715.4 cm² ; 1029 cm³
J: 102 m² ; 65 m³

Problem Solving

2 ; 3.5 ; 1.7
2 ; 3.5 ; 1.7 ; 5.5 ; 1.7 ; 4.675 ; 4.675

1. $3.8 \times 7.1 \div 2 = 13.49$; 13.49

2a. $4 \times 3 \div 2 = 6$; 6

b. Short base of garden: $8 - 3 - 1 = 4$
Long base of garden: $8 - 1 = 7$
Area of garden: $(4 + 7) \times 4 \div 2 = 22$
22

3a. $85.5 \div 9 = 9.5$
9.5

b. Short base of trapezoid: 9
Long base of trapezoid: $8 + 9 = 17$
Area: $(9 + 17) \times 9.5 \div 2 = 123.5$
123.5

4a. Side length: $1.8 \div 4 = 0.45$
Perimeter: $0.45 \times 6 = 2.7$
2.7

b. Area of 1 rhombus: $0.45 \times 0.5 = 0.225$
Area of 2 rhombuses: $0.225 \times 2 = 0.45$
0.45

5a. Base of triangle: $24 \div 2 = 12$
Height of triangle: $96 \times 2 \div 12 = 16$; 16

b. Height of larger triangle: $50 - 16 = 34$
Area of kite: $24 \times 34 \div 2 + 96 \times 2 = 600$
600

6a. $15 \times 15 \times 15 = 3375$
The volume is 3375 cm².

b. $15 \times 15 \times 6 = 1350$
1350 cm² of cardboard is needed.

7a. $(18.2 \times 10.5 \div 2) \times 10 = 955.5$
The volume of the gift box is 955.5 cm³.

b. $(18.2 \times 10.5 \div 2) \times 2 + 13.9 \times 10 \times 2 + 18.2 \times 10 = 651.1$
651.1 cm² of wrapping paper is needed.

8a. $(14 \times 14 \div 2) \times 15 = 1470$
The volume of Prism A is 1470 cm³.

b. Volume of Prism B: $1470 \times 2 = 2940$
Volume of entire prism: $1470 + 2940 = 4410$
Length of prism: $4410 \div 15 \div 14 = 21$
Surface area:
$14 \times 15 \times 2 + 14 \times 21 \times 2 + 15 \times 21 \times 2 = 1638$
The surface area is 1638 cm².

9a. $3 \times 2 \div (1 + 3) = 1.5$
The height of the ramp is 1.5 m.

b. $3 \times 2 + 1.5 \times 1 + 1 \times 1 + 2.5 \times 1 = 11$
11 m² will be painted.

10a. $13.5 \times 17 \div 2 \times 2 = 229.5$
The volume is 229.5 cm³.

b. Total height: $17 + 3 = 20$
Volume: $15 \times 20 \div 2 \times 2 = 300$
The volume is 300 cm³.

11a. Width of a step: $1.6 \div 4 = 0.4$
Height of a step: $0.8 \div 4 = 0.2$
Volume of 1 step: $0.4 \times 1.5 \times 0.2 = 0.12$
The volume of the staircase is the same as the volume of 10 steps.
Volume of staircase: $0.12 \times 10 = 1.2$
The volume of the staircase is 1.2 m³.

b. Area of trapezoid: $1.2 \div 1.2 = 1$
Sum of bases: $1 \times 2 \div 0.8 = 2.5$
Longer base: $2.5 - 0.4 = 2.1$
Difference: $2.1 - 1.6 = 0.5$
d is 0.5 m.

c. $2.2 \times 1.2 + 0.4 \times 1.2 = 3.12$
3.12 m² was painted.

12a. Side length: $15 - 5 = 10$
Volume: $10 \times 10 \times 10 = 1000$
The volume was 1000 cm³.

b. Surface area of design:
12 rectangular faces: $10 \times 5 \times 12 = 600$
8 square faces: $5 \times 5 \times 8 = 200$
Total: $600 + 200 = 800$
The surface area of the design is 800 cm².

ISBN: 978-1-77149-205-8

c. The centre of the design is a cube with a side length of 5 cm.
$5 \times 5 \times 5 = 125$ (cm³) $= 125$ (mL)
It can hold 125 mL of water.

13a. Volume of 1 triangular prism: $45.9 \div 2 = 22.95$
Area of triangle: $22.95 \div 10.2 = 2.25$
Height of triangle: $2.25 \times 2 \div 1.5 = 3$
The side length is 3 cm.

b. Longer base of trapezoid: $1.5 + 3 + 1.5 = 6$
Surface area: $(3 + 6) \times 3 \div 2 \times 2 + 6 \times 10.2 + 3.4 \times 10.2 \times 2 + 3 \times 10.2 = 188.16$
The surface area is 188.16 cm².

9   Angles

Math Skills

1. 30° ; 90°   2. 30° ; 60°
3. 50° ; 40°   4. 40° ; 140°
5. 124° ; 124° ; 124° ; 124°
6. 39° ; 141° ; 141° ; 39°
7. 38° ; 52° ; 38°   8. 45° ; 105° ; 75°

Problem Solving

50° ; 130° ; 50° ; 130° ; 130° ; 50° ; 130°

1. By angles in a triangle: $180° - 37° - 53° = 90°$
is

2a. By complementary angles: $90° - 29° = 61°$
61°

b. By angles in a triangle: $180° - 90° - 29° = 61°$
61°

c. By supplementary angles: $180° - 61° = 119°$
119°

3a. By angles in a triangle: $180° - 90° - 60° = 30°$
30°

b. By supplementary angles: $180° - 60° = 120°$
120°

4a. By complementary angles: $90° - 48° = 42°$
42°

b. By supplementary angles: $180° - 48° = 132°$
132°

c. By opposite angles: ∠ARB = 48°

∠ARC
= ∠ARB + ∠BRC
= 48° + 90°
= 138° ; 138°

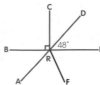

d. $132° \div 2 = 66°$; 66°

5a. By supplementary angles:
$180° - 37° - 37° = 106°$
The angle is 106°.

b. Sum of 2 angles: $180° - 128° = 52°$
Angle of reflection: $52° \div 2 = 26°$
The angle of reflection is 26°.

6a. By alternate angles: $i = 39°$; i is 39°.
b. By alternate angles: $j = 39°$; j is 39°.
c. Yes, the "W" is symmetrical because i and j are equal.

7a. No, they cannot be found. More information is needed.
b. Yes, the sum of the angles can be found. Each of the angles is equal to its opposite angle. By angles in a triangle, the sum of the angles must be 180°.

8a. Half of a is 67° by alternate angles due to symmetry.
$67° \times 2 = 134°$
a is 134°.

b. Half of a is a consecutive interior angle with b.
By consecutive interior angles:
$180° - 67° = 113°$
b is 113°.

9a. By consecutive interior angles:
$180° - 129° = 51°$
x is 51°.

b. By supplementary angles: $180° - 51° = 129°$
Raindrops will slide down the roof at an angle of 129°.

10a. By consecutive interior angles:
$180° - 59° = 121°$
s is 121°.

b. By alternate angles: $t = s = 121°$
t is 121°.

c. By angles in a triangle: $180° - 90° - 59° = 31°$
u is 31°.

d. (Suggested answer)
First find the consecutive interior angle to t which makes a 90° angle with u.
By consecutive interior angles:
$180° - 121° = 59°$
By complementary angles: $90° - 59° = 31°$
u is 31°.

11a. By corresponding angles: $g = 70°$
g is 70°.

b. By consecutive interior angles:
$180° - 70° = 110°$
By opposite angles: $h = 110°$
h is 110°.

c. By opposite angles: $i + g = 125°$
i: $125° - 70° = 55°$
i is 55°.

d. By consecutive interior angles:
$j + i + g = 180°$
j: $180° - 55° - 70° = 55°$
j is 55°.

ISBN: 978-1-77149-205-8

e-f.

The subway line bisects i at 27.5°.

g. By supplmentary angles:
180° – h = 180° – 110° = 70°
By angles in a triangle: 180° – 90° – 70° = 20°
The train track and 8th Ave. will intersect at an angle of 20°.

10 Cartesian Coordinate Plane

Math Skills

1. Parallelogram P: (-6,2), (-4,5), (-2,2), (0,5)
   Trapezoid T: (3,-3), (4,2), (6,-3), (6,2)

2.

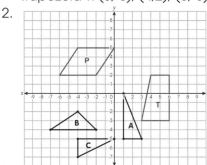

3a. (1,0)   b. (0,5), (0,-5)
4a. Triangles B and C
  b. Parallelogram P   c. Trapezoid T

Problem Solving

(-3,3) ; (-2,-2) ; (-1,-1)
2 ; 2 ; 3 ; 1

1. (2,-1) ; (3,-2) ; (1,-4)
2a. Larry: Shape B   Henry: Shape A
   Diana: Shape C
  b. Greatest x-coordinate: Diana's shape
   Smallest y-coordinate: Larry's shape

c.

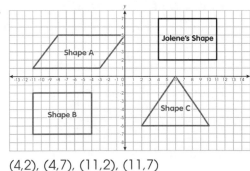

(4,2), (4,7), (11,2), (11,7)

3.

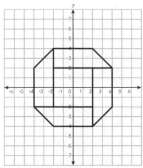

a. The shape is a trapezoid.
b. $\frac{1}{4}$ clockwise rotation about (0,0):
   (2,2), (2,-4), (4,2), (4,-2)
   $\frac{1}{2}$ rotation about (0,0):
   (-4,-2), (-2,-4), (2,-2), (2,-4)
   $\frac{1}{4}$ counterclockwise rotation about (0,0):
   (-4,2), (-4,-2), (-2,4), (-2,-2)
c. The order of rotational symmetry is 4.

4a-d.

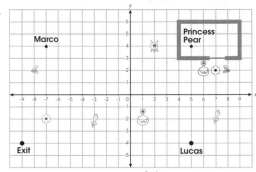

b. ✿ : (-7,-2)   : (2,4)
   ✎ : (-8,2)   : (1,-2)
c. Marco: Marco moved 4 units to the right and 6 units down.
   Lucas: Lucas moved 2 units to the right and 2 units up.
e. They moved 2 units to the right, 8 units down, and 16 units to the left.

5a.

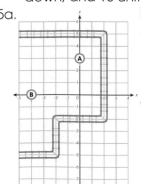

b. Jonas is at (4,-16).
c. Jonas should travel 3 units up, 8 units to the left, and 4 units up.
d. The train broke down at (2,0).

ISBN: 978-1-77149-205-8

6a.

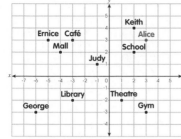

b. Keith lives closest to Alice. Alice should go 1 unit to the left and 1 unit up.

c. George's house is the farthest away.

d. (2,3) and (-4,1) could be part of the lake.

e. The gym is at (3,-3) and the café is at (-3,3).

f. George lives in the Town of Sunnyville.

g. Ernice and Judy live in the Town of Nightvale.

h. Ernice's house: the café and Alice's house
Keith's house: the school
The mall: the school
The theatre: the library

i. The possible coordinates of Bernard's house are (-1,3) and (3,1).

j. The park could be located in Quadrants II or IV.

11 Algebra

Math Skills

1. 4 ; 5
2. 2 ; 22
3. 2 ; 4
4. 12
5. 9
6. 3
7. 1
8. 14
9. 2
10. 1
11. 2
12. -1
13. 8.75
14. -10
15. 3
16. 0
17. 9.125
18. $3n = 6$
 $n = 2$
19. $a \div 2 = 5$
 $a = 10$
20. $2(x + 3) \div 2 = 10 \div 2$
 $x + 3 = 5$
 $x = 2$
21. $(b - 5) \div 2 \times 2 = 1 \times 2$
 $b - 5 = 2$
 $b = 7$
22. $\frac{z}{3} = 3$
 $\frac{z}{3} \times 3 = 3 \times 3$
 $z = 9$
23. $12y = 24$
 $y = 2$
24. $16m = 2m + 7$
 $16m - 2m = 2m + 7 - 2m$
 $14m = 7$
 $m = 0.5$
25. $2b = b - 15$
 $2b - b = b - 15 - b$
 $b = -15$

26. $3d - 9 = 4d + 2$
 $3d = 4d + 11$
 $3d - 4d = 4d + 11 - 4d$
 $-d = 11$
 $d = -11$

Problem Solving

7 ; 12 ; 13 ; 13

1. Let s be the cost of each sandwich.
 $2s + 4 = 16$
 $2s = 12$
 $s = 6$

6

2a. Let c be Cory's earnings each hour.
 $3 \times 6 \times c = 207$
 $18c = 207$
 $c = 11.5$

11.50

b. Let m be Melissa's earnings each hour.
 $m + 6 = 2 \times 11.5$
 $m + 6 = 23$
 $m = 17$

17

3. Let d be the distance hiked in the morning.
 $d + \frac{2}{3}d = 2$
 $1\frac{2}{3}d = 2$
 $d = 1\frac{1}{5}$

$1\frac{1}{5}$

4. 8 kg = 8000 g
 Let n be the number of cans.
 $16 \times n = 8000 \div 2$
 $16n = 4000$
 $n = 250$

250

5. Let s be the capacity of the smaller bottle.
 $3s + s = 2$
 $4s = 2$
 $s = 0.5$
 Larger bottle: $3 \times 0.5 = 1.5$

1.5 ; 0.5

6. Let b be the amount of broth in a can.
 $\frac{3}{4}b + 284 = 500$
 $\frac{3}{4}b = 216$
 $\frac{3}{4}b \div \frac{3}{4} = 216 \div \frac{3}{4}$
 $b = 288$

288

ISBN: 978-1-77149-205-8

7. Let h be the additional no. of half hours.
$$8 + 4.5h = 21.5$$
$$4.5h = 13.5$$
$$h = 3$$
Total time: $1 + 3 \times 0.5 = 2.5$
Brock rented the bike for 2.5 hours.

8. Let m be the number of minutes.
$$33m - 5m = 140$$
$$28m = 140$$
$$m = 5$$
It will take 5 minutes.

9a. Let s be Simon's age.
$$(3s - 4) + s = 44$$
$$4s - 4 = 44$$
$$4s = 48$$
$$s = 12$$
Simon is 12 years old.

b. Mr. Lohan's age: $3 \times 12 - 4 = 32$
Let y be the number of years.
$$2(12 + y) = 32 + y$$
$$24 + 2y = 32 + y$$
$$2y = y + 8$$
$$2y - y = y + 8 - y$$
$$y = 8$$
In 8 years, Mr. Lohan's age will be twice Simon's age.

10a. Let s be the cost of 1 slice of cake.
$$5s - 2s = 15.3$$
$$3s = 15.3$$
$$s = 5.1$$
The cost of 1 slice of cake is $5.10.

b. Let p be the price for each slice.
$$6p = 5 \times 5.1$$
$$6p = 25.5$$
$$p = 4.25$$
Linda paid $4.25 for each slice of cake.

11. Let j be the number of cookies in the jar.
$$j - \frac{1}{4}j - (\frac{1}{4}j - 3) = 15$$
$$j - \frac{1}{4}j - \frac{1}{4}j + 3 = 15$$
$$\frac{1}{2}j + 3 = 15$$
$$\frac{1}{2}j = 12$$
$$\frac{1}{2}j \times 2 = 12 \times 2$$
$$j = 24$$
There were 24 cookies in the jar.

12. Let w be the weight of an orange.
$$5(w - 52) = 3w$$
$$5w - 260 = 3w$$
$$5w - 3w = 260$$
$$2w = 260$$
$$w = 130$$
An orange weighs 130 g.

13a. Let s be the cost of a scarf.
$$2s + 3(s + 8) = 69$$
$$2s + 3s + 24 = 69$$
$$5s = 45$$
$$s = 9$$
Cost of a hat: $9 + $8 = $17
A scarf costs $9 and a hat costs $17.

b. $17 \times 2 + $9 \times 3 = $61
2 hats and 3 scarves cost $61.

14a. Let t be the no. of text messages Mia sent.
$$16.55 + 0.35t = 26$$
$$0.35t = 9.45$$
$$t = 27$$
Mia sent 27 text messages.

b. $$16.55 + 0.35t + 26 = 59$$
$$0.35t + 42.55 = 59$$
$$0.35t = 16.45$$
$$t = 47$$
Mia sent 47 text messages.

15. Let s be the savings on each pen.
$$12.54 = 6(2.3 - s)$$
$$12.54 = 13.8 - 6s$$
$$6s = 13.8 - 12.54$$
$$6s = 1.26$$
$$s = 0.21$$
$0.21 is saved on each pen.

16a. Let m be the number of seconds jogged.
$$30 + 8m = 110 + 3m$$
$$8m - 3m = 110 - 30$$
$$5m = 80$$
$$m = 16$$
After 16 seconds, Tracy and Jordan will have jogged the same distance.

b. $$30 + 8m = 2(110 + 3m)$$
$$30 + 8m = 220 + 6m$$
$$8m - 6m = 220 - 30$$
$$2m = 190$$
$$m = 95$$
It will take Jordan 95 minutes.

17a. Let s be the number of seconds needed to print in colour.
$$8(s - 2) + 6s = 54$$
$$8s - 16 + 6s = 54$$
$$14s = 70$$
$$s = 5$$
It took 5 seconds to print a page in colour.

b. Time needed to print in black and white:
$5 - 2 = 3$
Let p be the number of pages in the book.
$$3p + 5p = 160$$
$$8p = 160$$
$$p = 20$$
The book had 20 pages.

ISBN: 978-1-77149-205-8

18. Let x be the number of quarters.
$0.25x + 0.1(24 - x) = 3.45$
$0.25x + 2.4 - 0.1x = 3.45$
$0.15x = 3.45 - 2.4$
$0.15x = 1.05$
$x = 7$
Number of dimes: $24 - 7 = 17$
There are 7 quarters and 17 dimes.

12   Data Management

Math Skills

1a. 34 ; 33.5 ; 43   b. 140.9 ; 139.4 ; none
c. 12.95 ; 12.07 ; 8.33 and 19.45
2a. double line graph
Comparing 2 sets of continuous data requires a double line graph.
b. circle graph
An amount of time in a day is part of a whole.
c. histogram
The discrete data can be organized into continuous intervals.

Problem Solving

90° ; 25% ; 25% ; 75 ; 75
1a. Percent: $\frac{72°}{360°} \times 100\% = 20\%$
No. of people: $300 \times 20\% = 60$
60
b. Purple percent: $\frac{54°}{360°} \times 100\% = 15\%$
People who chose purple: $300 \times 15\% = 45$
Difference: $60 - 45 = 15$
15
2a. Chocolate flavoured:
$360 \times \frac{90°}{360°} = 90$
90 scoops were chocolate flavoured.
Caramel flavoured:
$360 \times \frac{60°}{360°} = 60$
60 scoops were caramel flavoured.
Mango flavoured:
$360 \times \frac{40°}{360°} = 40$
40 scoops were mango flavoured.
b. Half of the total number: $360 \div 2 = 180$
Strawberry: $360 \times \frac{120°}{360°} = 120$
Strawberry and caramel: $120 + 60 = 180$
Strawberry and caramel took up exactly half of the total number of scoops sold.
c. Strawberry was more popular.
$120 - 90 = 30$
30 more scoops were sold.

d. Vanilla had the fewest scoops sold.
Vanilla: $360 \times \frac{50°}{360°} = 50$
50 daily specials were sold at most.

3a.

Food Item	No. of Votes	Size of Angle
Pizza	48	$360° \times \frac{48}{120} = 144°$
Burger	30	$360° \times \frac{30}{120} = 90°$
Sandwich	24	$360° \times \frac{24}{120} = 72°$
Salad	12	$360° \times \frac{12}{120} = 36°$
Others	6	$360° \times \frac{6}{120} = 18°$

Students' Lunch Preferences

b. About 50% of all votes:
"Pizza" got about 50% of all votes.
Exactly 25% of all votes:
"Burger" got exactly 25% of all votes.
Twice as many votes as "Salad":
"Sandwich" got twice as many votes as "Salad".
Half as many votes as "Salad":
"Others" got half as many votes as "Salad".
c. (Suggested answer)
Yes, because each lunch preference is represented as part of a whole.
4a. GoldAir:
Mean: ($310 + $300 + $305 + $295 + $300 + $285 + $270) ÷ 7 = $295
Median: $300
Mode: $300
FlyWest:
Mean: ($260 + $275 + $275 + $290 + $290 + $300 + $305) ÷ 7 = $285
Median: $290
Mode: $275 and $290

b. GoldAir: The fare prices tended to decrease in later days in July.
FlyWest: The fare prices tended to increase in later days in July.
c. Rita booked with FlyWest for July 7.
5a. (Suggested answer)
The mean best describes this set of data because there are no values that are too small or too big in this set of data.
b. He should use Graph A. This is because the bars appear to be more uniform than Graph B.
c. He should use Graph B. This is because the bar in February is significantly longer than the other bars.

ISBN: 978-1-77149-205-8

d. (Individual answer)

6.

Heights of Plants (cm)

Stem	Leaf
0	3 4 6 8 9
1	0 2 3 3 3 6 9
2	1 1 1 4 8 9
3	2 2 5 6 8
4	0 2

key: 1|2 = 12 cm

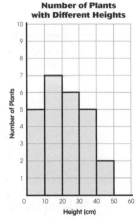

Number of Plants with Different Heights

a. There were 25 students in the class.

b. The tallest plant was 42 cm.
The shortest plant was 3 cm.

c. The 10 cm to 19 cm range had the most plants.
The 40 cm to 49 cm range had the fewest plants.

d. 10 cm to 29 cm range: 7 + 6 = 13
There were 13 plants.
Shorter than 40 cm: 5 + 7 + 6 + 5 = 23
There were 23 plants.
Taller than 19 cm: 6 + 5 + 2 = 13
There were 13 plants.

e. (3 + 4 + 6 + 8 + 9 + 10 + 12 + 13 + 13 + 13 + 16 + 19 + 21 + 21 + 21 + 24 + 28 + 29 + 32 + 32 + 35 + 36 + 38 + 40 + 42) ÷ 25 = 21
The mean height of the plants is 21 cm.

f. Median: 21 cm
The median height belongs in the 20 cm to 29 cm range.

g. Ben's plant is in the 10 cm to 19 cm range.

13 Probability

Math Skills

1a. $\frac{2}{8}$; 25   b. $\frac{1}{8}$; 12.5   c. $\frac{4}{8}$; 50%

d. $\frac{6}{8}$; 75%   e. $\frac{0}{8}$; 0%   f. $\frac{4}{8}$; 50%

g. $\frac{2}{8}$; 25%   h. $\frac{4}{8}$; 50%   i. $\frac{3}{8}$; 37.5%

j. $\frac{7}{8}$; 87.5%   k. $\frac{4}{8}$; 50%   l. $\frac{4}{8}$; 50%

2a. $\frac{1}{4}$; 25   b. $\frac{1}{4}$; 25%   c. $\frac{1}{2}$; 50%

d. $\frac{1}{2}$; 50%   e. $\frac{2}{4}$; 50%   f. $\frac{2}{2}$; 100%

g. $\frac{3}{4}$; 75%   h. $\frac{1}{4}$; $\frac{1}{2}$; $\frac{1}{8}$; 12.5%

i. $\frac{1}{4}$; $\frac{1}{2}$; $\frac{1}{8}$; 12.5%

Problem Solving

$\frac{1}{2}$; $\frac{1}{6}$; $\frac{1}{2}$; $\frac{1}{6}$; $\frac{1}{12}$; $\frac{1}{12}$

1. P(tails) = $\frac{1}{2}$
P(even number) = $\frac{3}{6}$ = $\frac{1}{2}$
P(tails and even number) = $\frac{1}{2}$ × $\frac{1}{2}$ = $\frac{1}{4}$
$\frac{1}{4}$

2. Way 1:
a. P([A]) = $\frac{1}{4}$ P(D) = $\frac{1}{4}$
P([A] and D) = $\frac{1}{4}$ × $\frac{1}{4}$ = $\frac{1}{16}$

b. P([B]) = $\frac{1}{4}$ P(C) = $\frac{1}{4}$
P([B] and C) = $\frac{1}{4}$ × $\frac{1}{4}$ = $\frac{1}{16}$

c. P([C]) = $\frac{1}{4}$ P(C) = $\frac{1}{4}$
P([C] and C) = $\frac{1}{4}$ × $\frac{1}{4}$ = $\frac{1}{16}$

Way 2:

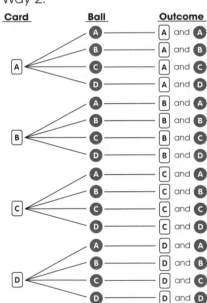

d. $\frac{1}{16}$ e. $\frac{1}{16}$ f. $\frac{1}{16}$

g. Yes, they are the same.
(Individual preference)

3a. • two "**1**":
P(**1** and **1**) = $\frac{1}{3}$ × $\frac{1}{2}$ = $\frac{1}{6}$
The probability is $\frac{1}{6}$.
• a sum of 5:
A sum of 5: **3** + **2**
P(**3** and **2**) = $\frac{1}{3}$ × $\frac{1}{2}$ = $\frac{1}{6}$
The probability is $\frac{1}{6}$.

ISBN: 978-1-77149-205-8

- two even numbers:
  Even numbers: **2** and **2**
  $P(\textbf{2} \text{ and } \textbf{2}) = \frac{1}{3} \times \frac{1}{2} = \frac{1}{6}$
  The probability is $\frac{1}{6}$.

b. • two "**1**": $60 \times \frac{1}{6} = 10$
  Michael will get two "**1**" about 10 times.

  • a sum of 5: $60 \times \frac{1}{6} = 10$
  Michael will get a sum of 5 about 10 times.

c. • two "**1**" ten times: $\frac{1}{6} = \frac{10}{60}$
  Michael spun the wheel about 60 times.

  • a sum of 5 ten times: $\frac{1}{6} = \frac{10}{60}$
  Michael spun the wheel about 60 times.

4a. • P(rolling two "3"):
  $\frac{1}{6} \times \frac{1}{6} = \frac{1}{36}$
  The probability is $\frac{1}{36}$.

  • P(rolling 2 numbers less than 5):
  P(rolling 1 number less than 5) $= \frac{4}{6} = \frac{2}{3}$
  P(rolling 2 numbers less than 5)
  $= \frac{2}{3} \times \frac{2}{3} = \frac{4}{9}$
  The probability is $\frac{4}{9}$.

  • P(rolling 2 even numbers):
  $\frac{1}{2} \times \frac{1}{2} = \frac{1}{4}$
  The probability is $\frac{1}{4}$.

  • P(rolling 2 of the same number):
  P(rolling any number) × P(rolling the same
  number again) $= \frac{6}{6} \times \frac{1}{6} = \frac{1}{6}$
  The probability is $\frac{1}{6}$.

b.

×	1	2	3	4	5	6
1	1	2	3	4	5	6
2	2	4	6	8	10	12
3	3	6	9	12	15	18
4	4	8	12	16	20	24
5	5	10	15	20	25	30
6	6	12	18	24	30	36

  • P(getting 36 as a product):
  The probability is $\frac{1}{36}$.

  • P(getting a perfect square as a product):
  Perfect squares: 1, 4, 9, 16, 25, 36
  $\frac{8}{36} = \frac{2}{9}$
  The probability is $\frac{2}{9}$.

c. $P(6) = \frac{1}{6}$
  P(a product of 36) = P(6 and 6)
  $= \frac{1}{6} \times \frac{1}{6} = \frac{1}{36}$
  The probability is $\frac{1}{36}$.

5a. $P(\text{large}) = \frac{1}{3}$ $P(\text{ginger ale}) = \frac{1}{2}$
  $P(\text{large ginger ale}) = \frac{1}{3} \times \frac{1}{2} = \frac{1}{6}$
  The probability is $\frac{1}{6}$.

b. $P(\text{small}) = \frac{1}{3}$ $P(\text{lemonade}) = \frac{1}{2}$
  $P(\text{small lemonade}) = \frac{1}{3} \times \frac{1}{2} = \frac{1}{6}$
  The probability is $\frac{1}{6}$.

c. P(not small lemonade)
  $= 1 - P(\text{small lemonade}) = 1 - \frac{1}{6} = \frac{5}{6}$
  The probability is $\frac{5}{6}$.

d. $P(\text{vanilla}) = \frac{1}{3}$ $P(\text{waffle cone}) = \frac{1}{2}$
  $P(\text{sprinkles}) = \frac{1}{2}$
  P(vanilla, waffle cone, sprinkles)
  $= \frac{1}{3} \times \frac{1}{2} \times \frac{1}{2} = \frac{1}{12}$
  The probability is $\frac{1}{12}$.

e. $P(\text{not}) = 1 - \frac{1}{12} = \frac{11}{12}$
  Frequency: $60 \times \frac{11}{12} = 55$
  About 55 ice cream cones were not vanilla
  ice cream in waffle cones with sprinkles.

6. Marbles in the box: 5 white, 15 black
  Marbles in the bag: 15 white, 5 black

a. • 2 black marbles:
  P(black marble from box) $= \frac{15}{20} = \frac{3}{4}$
  P(black marble from bag) $= \frac{5}{20} = \frac{1}{4}$
  P(2 black marbles) $= \frac{3}{4} \times \frac{1}{4} = \frac{3}{16}$
  The probability is $\frac{3}{16}$.

  • a white marble from the box and a black
  marble from the bag:
  P(white marble from box) $= \frac{5}{20} = \frac{1}{4}$
  P(black marble from bag) $= \frac{5}{20} = \frac{1}{4}$
  P(white marble from box, black marble
  from bag) $= \frac{1}{4} \times \frac{1}{4} = \frac{1}{16}$
  The probability is $\frac{1}{16}$.

  • a black marble from the box and a white
  marble from the bag:
  P(black marble from box) $= \frac{15}{20} = \frac{3}{4}$
  P(white marble from bag) $= \frac{15}{20} = \frac{3}{4}$
  P(black marble from box, white marble
  from bag) $= \frac{3}{4} \times \frac{3}{4} = \frac{9}{16}$
  The probability is $\frac{9}{16}$.

ISBN: 978-1-77149-205-8

- a white marble and a black marble:
  P(white and black marbles)
  = P(white marble from box, black marble from bag) + P(black marble from box, white marble from bag)
  $= \frac{1}{16} + \frac{9}{16} = \frac{10}{16} = \frac{5}{8}$

  The probability is $\frac{5}{8}$.

b. $40 \times \frac{5}{8} = 25$

  Linda will get a white marble and a black marble about 25 times.

7a. There are 5 outcomes from the 1st pick and 5 outcomes from the 2nd pick.
  $5 \times 5 = 25$
  There are 25 possible outcomes.

b. • both cards will be "A":
  $P(2\text{ "A"}) = \frac{1}{5} \times \frac{1}{5} = \frac{1}{25}$

  The probability is $\frac{1}{25}$.

  • both cards will be vowels:
  Vowels: A, E
  $P(2\text{ vowels}) = \frac{2}{5} \times \frac{2}{5} = \frac{4}{25}$

  The probability is $\frac{4}{25}$.

  • none of the cards will be vowels:
  $P(\text{no vowels}) = \frac{3}{5} \times \frac{3}{5} = \frac{9}{25}$

  The probability is $\frac{9}{25}$.

  • none of the cards will be a "B":
  $P(\text{no "B"}) = \frac{4}{5} \times \frac{4}{5} = \frac{16}{25}$

  The probability is $\frac{16}{25}$.

c. • both cards be "A":
  $50 \times \frac{1}{25} = 2$
  Both cards will be "A" about 2 times.

  • both cards be vowels:
  $50 \times \frac{4}{25} = 8$
  Both cards will be vowels about 8 times.

Critical-thinking Questions

Unit 1

1. $15.68 \times 12.5 = 196$; $\sqrt{196} = 14$; $14 \times 4 = 56$;
   56 cm

2. Let q be the number of quarters.
   $0.05 \times 2q + 0.1 \times \frac{1}{4}q + 0.25q = 37.5$
   $\qquad\qquad\qquad 0.375q = 37.5$
   $\qquad\qquad\qquad\qquad q = 100$
   Money in quarters: $\$0.25 \times 100 = \$25$

Fraction in quarters: $\frac{25}{37.5} = \frac{250}{375} = \frac{2}{3}$
$\frac{2}{3}$ of Alyssa's money is in quarters.

3. By supplementary angles: $a + b = 180°$
   $a{:}b{:}a{+}b = 3{:}2{:}5 = 108°{:}72°{:}180°$
   By supplementary angles: $d + e = 180°$
   $d{:}e{:}d{+}e = 4{:}5{:}9 = 80°{:}100°{:}180°$
   By angles in a triangle: $b + c + d = 180°$
   $\qquad\qquad 72° + c + 80° = 180°$
   $\qquad\qquad\qquad\qquad\qquad c = 28°$

   c is 28°.

4. Side length of small tile: $\sqrt{144} = 12$
   Side length of big tile: $\sqrt{225} = 15$
   LCM of 12 and 15: 60
   Area of square floor: $60 \times 60 = 3600$
   No. of small tiles: $3600 \div 144 = 25$
   No. of big tiles: $3600 \div 225 = 16$
   Difference: $25 - 16 = 9$
   The smallest possible area is 3600 cm².
   9 more small tiles than big tiles are needed.

5.

×	-5	-2	3
-5	25	10	-15
-2	10	4	-6
3	-15	-6	9

   Probability: $\frac{4}{9}$
   The probability is $\frac{4}{9}$.

6. Area to be painted:
   $75 \times 60 \times 2 + 60 \times 40 \times 2 + 75 \times 40 = 16\ 800$
   Paint needed:
   $16\ 800 \div 10 \times 2 = 3360$ (mL) = 3.36 (L)
   No. of cans: $3.36 \div 2.4 = 1.4$
   Kaitlyn will use 1.4 cans of paint.

7. Old fish tank: $4{:}3{:}6 = 24{:}18{:}36$
   New length: $24 + 24 \times 50\% = 36$
   New width: $18 + 18 \times 50\% = 27$
   New height: $36 + 36 \times 50\% = 54$
   New capacity: $36 \times 27 \times 54 = 52\ 488$
   The capacity is 52 488 mL.

8. Perfect squares less than 240:
   1, 4, 9, 16, 25, 36, 49, 64, 81, 100, 121, 144, 169, 196, 225
   Probability of 1 person: $\frac{15}{240} = \frac{1}{16}$
   Probability of 2 people: $\frac{1}{16} \times \frac{1}{16} = \frac{1}{256}$
   The probability is $\frac{1}{256}$.

9. Let f be the original fish population.
   $f + \frac{3}{4}f + \frac{3}{4}(f + \frac{3}{4}f) = 245$
   $f + \frac{3}{4}f + \frac{3}{4}f + \frac{9}{16}f = 245$
   $\qquad\qquad\qquad 3\frac{1}{16}f = 245$
   $\qquad\qquad\qquad\qquad f = 80$
   The original fish population was 80.

ISBN: 978-1-77149-205-8

10. Let t be the number of seconds needed.

$$3.41 \div 5.5 \times t - 1.71 \div 4.5 \times t = 180$$
$$0.62t - 0.38t = 180$$
$$0.24t = 180$$
$$t = 750$$

It will take 750 s for the tank to be full.

11.

Angle of vanilla: $180° - 90° = 90°$
(by supplementary angles)

lemon:mint:lemon and mint
$= 1:2:3 = 30°:60°:90°$
(1+2) (by complementary angles)

Angle of strawberry: $60°$
Angle of chocolate: $180° - 60° = 120°$
(by supplementary angles)

Total cones sold: $72 \div \dfrac{90°}{360°} = 288$

Chocolate sold: $288 \times \dfrac{120°}{360°} = 96$

96 chocolate flavoured ice cream cones were sold.

12. Strawberry sold: $(288 \div 2) - 96 = 48$
Total revenue: $\$5.50 \times (96 + 72 + 48) + \$6.25 \times (288 - 96 - 72 - 48) = \$1638$
Revenue from chocolate and vanilla:
$\$5.50 \times (96 + 72) = \$924$
Percent: $\$924 \div \$1638 = 56.4\%$
56.4% of the revenue came from the sales of the chocolate and vanilla flavours.

13. Let r be the annual interest rate.
$$2000 + 2000 \times r + 2000 \times r = 2200$$
$$2000 \times r + 2000 \times r = 200$$
$$4000 \times r = 200$$
$$r = 0.05$$
The annual interest rate was 5%.

14. Volume from 1 worker: $2 \times 3 \times 4 = 24$
Volume needed: $1.5 \times 6 \times 8 = 72$
No. of hours: $72 \div 24 \div 2 = 1.5$
1.5 hours are needed.

15. New score needed: $80\% \times 6 - 78\% \times 5 = 90\%$
New score: $20 \times 90\% = 18$
Roy must get 18 marks out of 20.

16.

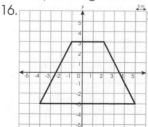

Long base: $5 \times 9 = 45$
Short base: $5 \times 3 = 15$
Height: $5 \times 6 = 30$
Area:
$(45 + 15) \times 30 \div 2 = 900$
The area of the farm is 900 m².

17. Probability of 1 bone: $\dfrac{7}{28} = \dfrac{1}{4}$

Probability of both bones: $\dfrac{1}{4} \times \dfrac{1}{4} = \dfrac{1}{16}$

The probability is $\dfrac{1}{16}$.

18. GCF of 36 and 48: 12

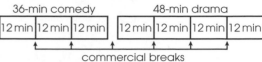

Total commercial time:
1 h 36 min – 36 min – 48 min = 12 min
Time of each commercial break: $12 \div 6 = 2$
Each commercial break is 2 min long at most.

19. By consecutive interior angles:
$\angle DBA + \angle BAC = 180°$
$\angle DBA : \angle BAC : \angle DBA + \angle BAC$
$= 2:1:3 = 120°:60°:180°$
By angles in a triangle:
$\angle BOD + 60° + 90° = 180°$
$\angle BOD = 30°$
The size of $\angle BOD$ would be $30°$.

20.

Overlapped base: $2 \times 1 = 2$
Overlapped height: $2 \times 2 = 4$
Overlapped area: $2 \times 4 \div 2 = 4$
The coordinates of the vertices of the image are (-3,-1), (-3,-7), and (-6,-7). The area of the overlapped section is 4 cm².

Unit 2

1. $\left(2\dfrac{4}{9} + 4\dfrac{2}{9}\right) \times 4\dfrac{1}{5} \div 2 = 14$; $14 \div 6\dfrac{2}{3} = 2\dfrac{1}{10}$;
$2\dfrac{1}{10}$ m²/min

2. Let w be the amount of milk added.
$$(50 + w) \times 25\% = 50 \times 80\%$$
$$12.5 + 0.25w = 40$$
$$0.25w = 27.5$$
$$w = 110$$
110 mL of milk should be added.

3. $5:6:9:20 = 64:76.8:115.2:256$
(×12.8 over (5+6+9))
Side length of square lid: $64 \div 4 = 16$
Area of lid: $16^2 = 256$
The area of the lid is 256 cm².

ISBN: 978-1-77149-205-8

4. Mean speed: $(95 \times 4 + 102 \times 3) \div 7 = 98$
 Median speed: 95 95 95 ⑨⑤ 102 102 102
 Erica's mean speed was 98 km/h and her median speed was 95 km/h.

5. Height: $\frac{1}{2} + \frac{1}{4} = \frac{3}{4}$
 Surface area: $\frac{1}{2} \times \frac{1}{4} \times 2 + \frac{1}{2} \times \frac{3}{4} \times 2 +$
 $\frac{1}{4} \times \frac{3}{4} \times 2 = \frac{1}{4} + \frac{3}{4} + \frac{3}{8} = 1\frac{3}{8}$
 The surface area is $1\frac{3}{8}$ m².

6. Let x be the number of dimes.
 $5.65 = 0.1x + 0.25(25 - x)$
 $5.65 = 0.1x + 6.25 - 0.25x$
 $0.15x = 0.6$
 $x = 4$
 Quarters: $25 - 4 = 21$
 John has 4 dimes and 21 quarters.

7. Side length of cube: $\sqrt{169} = 13$
 Volume of 6 cubes: $13 \times 13 \times 13 \times 6 = 13\,182$
 The volume is 13 182 cm³.

8. Factors of 12: 1, 2, 3, 4, 6, 12
 Factors of 20: 1, 2, 4, 5, 10, 20
 Common factors of 12 and 20: 1, 2, 4
 Probability: $\frac{3}{12} \times \frac{3}{20} = \frac{3}{80}$
 The probability is $\frac{3}{80}$.

9. By corresponding angles: $a = c$
 By supplementary angles:
 $b + 90° + c = 180°$
 $b + a = 90°$ $(a = c)$
 $2a = 90°$ $(a = b)$
 $a = 45°$
 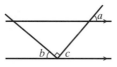
 The sizes of a and b are 45°.

10. $(4.8 + b) \times 3.6 \div 2 \times 2.5 = 50.4$
 $4.8 + b = 11.2$
 $b = 6.4$
 The length of the longer base, b, is 6.4 cm.

11. Mean temperature of Toronto:
 $(8 + 4 + (-2) + (-1) + 2 + 4 + 6) \div 7 = 3$
 Mean temperature of Calgary:
 $((-1) + (-5) + (-6) + (-4) + (-1) + 0 + 3) \div 7 = -2$
 Difference: $3 - (-2) = 5$
 The mean temperature of Toronto was 5°C warmer than Calgary's.

12. Let y be the mean temperature of Yellowknife.
 $\frac{1}{2}y = 4 \times (2 \times (-2) + \frac{1}{2} \times 3)$
 $\frac{1}{2}y = 4 \times (-2\frac{1}{2})$
 $\frac{1}{2}y = -10$
 $y = -20$
 The mean temperature of Yellowknife last week was -20°C.

13. By alternate angles:
 $\angle BAC = \angle DEC, \angle ABC = \angle EDC$
 By opposite angles: $\angle ACB = \angle ECD$
 $\overline{AB}:\overline{DE} = \overline{BC}:\overline{CD}$
 $4:6 = \overline{BC}:9$
 $\overline{BC} = 6$
 Distance from B to D: $6 + 9 = 15$
 Yes, it is possible. Priscilla walked 15 m.

14. Let t be the percent of tax.
 $((40.5 - 40.5 \times 20\%) + (56 - 56 \times 15\%)) \times (1 + t) = 88$
 $80 \times (1 + t) = 88$
 $1 + t = 1.1$
 $t = 0.1$
 Janice paid a 10% tax.

15. Let s be the side length.
 $6s^2 = 864$
 $s^2 = 144$
 $\sqrt{s^2} = \sqrt{144}$
 $s = 12$
 The side length of the cube is 12 cm.

16.
 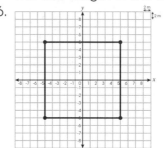
 Side length of enclosed area in Quadrant III: $2 \times 5 = 10$
 Area: $10 \times 10 = 100$
 The area is 100 m².

17. Fencing of enclosed area: 40 units
 Fencing of Quadrant III: 10 units
 $\frac{10}{40} = \frac{1}{4}$; The probability is $\frac{1}{4}$.

18. Side length of second layer: $\sqrt{196} = 14$
 $5:7:9 = 10:14:18$ ($\times 2$)
 Total volume of cake:
 $10 \times 10 \times 5 + 14 \times 14 \times 5 + 18 \times 18 \times 5 = 3100$
 The volume of the entire cake is 3100 cm³.

19. Sum of angles in 1 triangle: 180°
 Sum of angles in 8 triangles: $180° \times 8 = 1440°$
 Size of an angle in a regular decagon:
 $1440° \div 10 = 144°$ ← 144 is a perfect square.
 Yes, they are perfect squares.

20. Perimeters: $24 \times 4 = 96$; $36 \times 4 = 144$
 LCM of 96 and 144: 288
 Distance travelled after meeting 10 times:
 $288 \times 10 = 2880$
 Time: $2880 \div 15 = 192$
 It will take 192 seconds.

ISBN: 978-1-77149-205-8

Unit 3

1. $\$12.40 + \$12.40 \times 13\% = \$14.01$;
   $\$14.01 + \$14.01 \times 18.5\% = \$16.60$;
   $\$20 - \$16.60 = \$3.40$; $\$3.40$

2. Base of picture: $\sqrt{169} = 13$
   Base of frame: $13 + 1.5 + 1.5 = 16$
   Height of frame: $13 + 1.5 + 1.5 = 16$
   Area of frame: $16 \times 16 = 256$
   Area of border: $256 - 169 = 87$
   The area of the border is 87 cm².

3. Let w be the number of candies Woody had.
   $$w - 20 = 50\% \times w + 20$$
   $$50\% \times w = 40$$
   $$w = 80$$
   Woody had 80 candies originally.

4. By angles in a triangle:
   $x = 180° - 73° - 43.5° = 63.5°$
   By opposite angles:
   $y = x = 63.5°$
   By isosceles triangle:
   $z = y = 63.5°$
   By angles in a triangle:
   $a = 180° - 63.5° - 63.5° = 53°$
   No, Tim is incorrect. The largest angle is 73°.

5. Probability: $\dfrac{1}{2 + 3 + 1} = \dfrac{1}{6}$
   Total tokens: $18 \div \dfrac{1}{6} = 108$
   The probability is $\dfrac{1}{6}$. About 108 tokens have been thrown.

6. Let a be the glasses of apple juice sold and p be the glasses of pineapple juice sold.
   $5.25a = 441 \times \dfrac{1}{4}$ $6.75p = 441 \times \dfrac{3}{4}$
   $5.25a = 110.25$ $6.75p = 330.75$
   $a = 21$ $p = 49$
   Total: $21 + 49 = 70$
   70 glasses of juice were sold.

7. $1:2 = 12.5:25$ (×12.5)
   Surface area: $(25 + 12.5) \times 20 \div 2 \times 2 + 25 \times 7 + 20 \times 7 + 12.5 \times 7 + 23.6 \times 7 = 1317.7$
   1317.7 cm² of wrapping paper is needed.

8. Younger than 30: $30 + 50 + 60 = 140$
   Older than 50: 10
   Total passengers:
   $30 + 50 + 60 + 30 + 20 + 10 = 200$
   Difference: $140 - 10 = 130$
   Difference in percent: $130 \div 200 = 65\%$
   65% more passengers were younger than 30 than those who were older than 50.

9. Over 40: $\dfrac{20 + 10}{200} = 15\%$
   Probability: $10\% \times 15\% = 1.5\%$
   The probability was 1.5%.

10. No. of passengers in first class:
    $200 \times 10\% = 20$
    No. of passengers in economy class:
    $200 - 20 = 180$
    Let e be the cost of an economy ticket.
    $$20(e + 650) + 180e = 1625 \times 200$$
    $$20e + 13\,000 + 180e = 325\,000$$
    $$200e = 312\,000$$
    $$e = 1560$$
    An economy ticket cost $1560.

11. 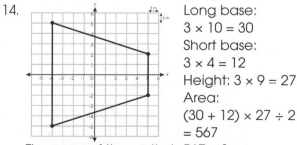 By consecutive interior angles: $a + b = 180°$
    Use the guess-and-check method.

a	b	
$4^2 = 16$	$180 - 16 = 164$	✗ not perfect square
$5^2 = 25$	$180 - 25 = 155$	✗
$6^2 = 36$	$180 - 36 = 144$	✔

    The angles are 36°, 144°, 36°, and 144°.

12. GCF of 45, 54, and 72: 9
    Volume of cardboard box:
    $72 \times 54 \times 45 = 174\,960$
    Volume of 1 cube-shaped box:
    $9 \times 9 \times 9 = 729$
    No. of snow globes: $174\,960 \div 729 = 240$
    There are at least 240 snow globes.

13. Let m be the temperature on Monday.
    $$m + (m - 1) + (m - 1 + 5) = (-2) \times 3$$
    $$3m + 3 = -6$$
    $$3m = -9$$
    $$m = -3$$
    The temperature on Monday was -3°C.

14. Long base:
    $3 \times 10 = 30$
    Short base:
    $3 \times 4 = 12$
    Height: $3 \times 9 = 27$
    Area:
    $(30 + 12) \times 27 \div 2$
    $= 567$
    The area of the patio is 567 m².

15. Possible coordinates:
    (-4,1) (-3,1) (-2,1) (-1,1)
    (-4,2) (-3,2) (-2,2) (-1,2)
    (-4,3) (-3,3) (-2,3) (-1,3)
    (-4,4) (-3,4) (-2,4) (-1,4)
    (-4,5)
    Only -4 and 1 have a sum of -3.
    The coordinates of the treasure are (-4,1).

ISBN: 978-1-77149-205-8

16. Area of patio: 5 + 164 = 169
    Side length of patio: $\sqrt{169}$ = 13
    Perimeter of patio: 13 × 4 = 52
    The perimeter of the patio is 52 m.

17. tomatoes:cucumbers:lettuce:salad
    $1\frac{2}{3} : 1\frac{5}{6} : 1\frac{1}{2} : 5$ = 300 : 330 : 270 : 900
    (×180, ($1\frac{2}{3}+1\frac{5}{6}+1\frac{1}{2}$))
    The weights are 300 g, 330 g, and 270 g for tomatoes, cucumbers, and lettuce respectively.

18. LCM of 12 and 16: 48
    Larry bought 48 pencils and 48 erasers.
    Let p be the number of pencils used.
    $p + \frac{1}{3}p = 44$
    $1\frac{1}{3}p = 44$
    $p = 33$
    No. of pencils left: 48 − 33 = 15
    15 pencils are left.

19.

×	-1	-3	2	1
5	(-1)×5 =-5	(-3)×5 =-15	2×5 =10	1×5 =5
-2	(-1)×(-2) = 2	(-3)×(-2) =6	2×(-2) =-4	1×(-2) =-2
4	(-1)×4 =-4	(-3)×4 =-12	2×4 =8	1×4 =4

▨ = negative product

Probability: $\frac{6}{12} = \frac{1}{2}$
The probability is $\frac{1}{2}$.

20. x:y:z:sum =3:2:1:6 = 90°:60°:30°:180°
    (×30, (3+2+1))
    Bisected x: 90° ÷ 2 = 45°
    Bisected y: 60° ÷ 2 = 30°
    By angles in a triangle:
    a = 180° − 45° − 30° = 105°
    a is 105°.

Unit 4

1. 5 × 5 × 2 + 5 × 8 × 4 = 210
   $0.001 × 210 = $0.21
   5 × 5 × 8 = 200
   $0.002 × 200 = $0.40
   $0.21 + $0.40 = $0.61 ; $0.61

2. $\frac{1}{3}$h = 20 min ; $\frac{3}{5}$h = 36 min ; $\frac{2}{5}$h = 24 min
   LCM of 20, 24, and 36: 360
   360 min = 6 h
   Next ring: 10:00 a.m. + 6 h = 4:00 p.m.
   The bells will all ring at 4:00 p.m.

3. Let r be the simple interest rate.
   4500 + 4500 × r × 5 = 4950
   22 500r = 450
   r = 0.02
   The simple interest rate was 2%.

4. The angles are equal by opposite angles and corresponding angles.

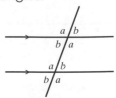

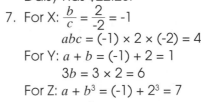

✔ = same angle

Probability: $\frac{8}{16} = \frac{1}{2}$
The probability is $\frac{1}{2}$.

5. red:blue:green:total
   = 2:3:10:15 = 48:72:240:360
   (×24, (2+3+10))
   GCF of 48, 72, and 240: 24
   There will be 24 kg of beads in each bag at most.

6. Let t be the number of toonies.
   $t + \frac{3}{4}t + \frac{3}{4}t - 5 = 15$
   $2\frac{1}{2}t = 20$
   $t = 8$
   Money: $2 × 8 + $1 × 8 × $\frac{3}{4}$ + $0.25 × (8 × $\frac{3}{4}$ − 5) = $22.25
   Daisy has $22.25.

7. For X: $\frac{b}{c} = \frac{2}{-2}$ = -1
   abc = (-1) × 2 × (-2) = 4
   For Y: $a + b$ = (-1) + 2 = 1
   $3b$ = 3 × 2 = 6
   For Z: $a + b^3$ = (-1) + 2^3 = 7
   a = -1

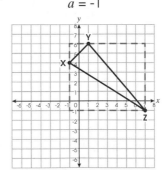

The locations of the radio towers are (-1,4), (1,6), and (7,-1).

8. No. of square units in triangle:
   8 × 7 − 8 × 5 ÷ 2 − 2 × 2 ÷ 2 − 6 × 7 ÷ 2 = 13
   Area of a square unit: 832 ÷ 13 = 64
   Side length of each square unit: $\sqrt{64}$ = 8
   The side length of each square is 8 km.

9. 1.5:0.7 = 100.5:46.9
   (×67)
   The length of the shadow would be 46.9 m.

10. $\frac{1}{3}$ × 1.2 × 2 + $\frac{1}{3}$ × $\frac{3}{4}$ × 2 + 1.2 × $\frac{3}{4}$ × 2 = 3.1
    Amy needs 3.1 m² of wrapping paper.

ISBN: 978-1-77149-205-8

11. Let s be the amount of syrup to be added.

$$240 \times 30\% + s = (240 + s) \times 40\%$$
$$72 + s = 96 + 0.4s$$
$$0.6s = 24$$
$$s = 40$$

Vanessa should add 40 mL of syrup.

12. Watched "The Forest Book": $\frac{72°}{360°} = \frac{1}{5}$

Liked "The Forest Book": $\frac{1}{5} \times \frac{3}{4} = \frac{3}{20}$

$\frac{3}{20}$ of the people surveyed liked it.

13. Fraction of "Decoy Prime": $\frac{36°}{360°} = \frac{1}{10}$

No. of people surveyed: $300 \div \frac{1}{10} = 3000$

No. of people who watched "Finding Dora":
$3000 \times \frac{108°}{360°} = 900$

No. of people who watched "Urban Battle":
$3000 \times \frac{54°}{360°} = 450$

Difference: $900 - 450 = 450$

450 more people watched "Finding Dora" than "Urban Battle".

14. Fraction of "Wild Borough": $\frac{90°}{360°} = \frac{1}{4}$

Probability: $\frac{1}{4} \times \frac{1}{3} = \frac{1}{12}$

The probability was $\frac{1}{12}$.

15. Volume of butter: $12 \times 4 \times 4 = 192$

Volume cut: $192 \times 20\% = 38.4$

Base of triangular face:
$38.4 \div 4 \times 2 \div 4 = 4.8$

Surface area of remaining butter:
$(12 + 12 - 4.8) \times 4 \div 2 \times 2 + 12 \times 4 + 4 \times 4 +$
$(12 - 4.8) \times 4 + 6.25 \times 4 = 194.6$

The surface area is 194.6 cm².

16. By opposite angles: $c = 144°$

$a{:}b{:}c{:}d = 4{:}3{:}6{:}2 = 96°{:}72°{:}144°{:}48°$

a, b, c, and d are 96°, 72°, 144°, and 48° respectively.

17. Distance to the left: $200 \times 10 = 2000$

No. of units to the left: $2000 \div 250 = 8$

Distance down: $100 \times 10 = 1000$

No. of units down: $1000 \div 250 = 4$

Mikayla moves 8 units to the left and 4 units down from (5,6).

Mikayla's location will be (-3,2).

18. P(red and then blue) = P(red) × P(blue)

Let p be the probability of picking a blue card.

$$\frac{3}{10} \times p = \frac{3}{20}$$
$$p = \frac{5}{10} \leftarrow \text{This implies that there are 5 blue cards.}$$

No. of black cards: $10 - 3 - 5 = 2$

There are 2 black cards.

19. Let s be the original price.

$$s \times (1 - 50\%) \times (1 - 20\%) = 6.24$$
$$s \times 0.5 \times 0.8 = 6.24$$
$$s = 15.6$$

Money saved: $\$15.60 - \$6.24 = \$9.36$

Michael saved $9.36.

20. $(\frac{3}{4} + 1\frac{7}{8}) \times 1\frac{2}{5} \div 2 \times 2\frac{2}{3} = 4\frac{9}{10}$

The volume of the tent is $4\frac{9}{10}$ m³.

Unit 5

1. 16 ; $\sqrt{16} = 4$; $4 \times 4 = 16$;
$144 \div 16 + 256 \div 16 = 25$; 16 cm ; 25

2. Let g be the number of girls.

$$\frac{3}{4}g = \frac{2}{5}(g + 7)$$
$$\frac{3}{4}g = \frac{2}{5}g + \frac{14}{5}$$
$$\frac{7}{20}g = \frac{14}{5}$$
$$g = 8$$

Total students: $8 + 8 + 7 = 23$

Probability: $\frac{8}{23}$

There are 8 girls. The probability is $\frac{8}{23}$.

3. Today's temperature: $(-18) \times 80\% = -14.4$

Temperature change: $(-14.4) - (-18) = 3.6$

The change in temperature is 3.6°C.

4. $36 = 2 \times 2 \times 3 \times 3 = 2^2 \times 3^2 = 4 \times 9$

The perfect squares are 4 and 9.

5. Let w be the width of the window.

$$6w \times 3w = 11\,250$$
$$18w^2 = 11\,250$$
$$w^2 = 625$$
$$w = 25$$

Area of window: $2 \times 25 \times 25 = 1250$

The area of the window is 1250 cm².

6. P(2 red marbles): $\frac{1}{4} = \frac{1}{2} \times \frac{1}{2}$

P(1 red marble): $\frac{1}{2}$

P(1 blue marble): $1 - \frac{1}{2} = \frac{1}{2}$

We can learn from the probabilities that the number of red marbles and the number of blue marbles are the same. So, the ratio of red to blue marbles is 1:1.

7. Let a be the number of years.

$$670 + 2 \times (670 \times 7\% \times a) = 1045.2$$
$$93.8a = 375.2$$
$$a = 4$$

It will take her 4 years.

ISBN: 978-1-77149-205-8

8.

Mary						
–	1	2	3	4	5	6
1	0	1	2	3	4	5
2	-1	0	1	2	3	4
3	-2	-1	0	1	2	3
4	-3	-2	-1	0	1	2
5	-4	-3	-2	-1	0	1
6	-5	-4	-3	-2	-1	0

(Perry on left axis)

▨ : less than -2

Probability: $\frac{6}{36} = \frac{1}{6}$

The probability is $\frac{1}{6}$.

9. By consecutive interior angles:
$d + a = 180°$
$c + b = 180°$
$d:a:d + a = 3:5:8 = 67.5°:112.5°:180°$ (×22.5, (3+5))
$c:b:c + b = 3:2:5 = 108°:72°:180°$ (×36, (3+2))
a is 112.5°, b is 72°, c is 108°, and d is 67.5°.

10. Capacity of new water bottle:
$1.28 + 1.28 × 30\% = 1.664$
Amount of water: $1.664 × \frac{7}{8} = 1.456$
There is 1.456 L of water.

11. x-coordinate:
$3(x – 2) = x + 2$
$3x – 6 = x + 2$
$2x = 8$
$x = 4$

y-coordinate:
$\frac{y}{-3} = (-2)^2 – 5$
$\frac{y}{-3} = -1$
$y = 3$

Leon is at (4,3). He is in Quadrant I.

12.

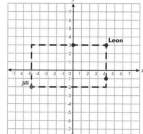

Jill is 14 units from Leon.
Distance to Ivan: $14 × \frac{5}{7} = 10$
Ivan's possible locations are (0,3) and (4,-1).

13. Volume of cut-out:
$12 × 12 × 12 – 1536 = 192$
Area of square base:
$192 ÷ 12 = 16$
Side length of square base: $\sqrt{16} = 4$
Surface area: $4 × 4 × 2 + 4 × 12 × 4 = 224$
The surface area of the cut-out is 224 cm².

14. Sports magazines: $1 – \frac{1}{3} – \frac{1}{5} = \frac{7}{15}$
Probability: $\frac{7}{15} × \frac{7}{15} = \frac{49}{225}$
The probability is $\frac{49}{225}$.

15. $1:1\frac{2}{3} = 3:5$
$1:1\frac{2}{3} = 4:6\frac{2}{3}$
$1:1\frac{2}{3} = 5:8\frac{1}{3}$
Area: $(3 + 8\frac{1}{3}) × 4 ÷ 2 = 22\frac{2}{3}$
Perimeter: $3 + 4 + 6\frac{2}{3} + 8\frac{1}{3} = 22$
The area is $22\frac{2}{3}$ cm² and the perimeter is 22 cm.

16. $\frac{3}{4} = 75\%$ ← range of 60% to 80%
4 other students are in the same range as Robert.

17. Total students: $4 + 6 + 3 + 5 + 7 = 25$
48% of students: $25 × 48\% = 12$
The top 12 students are in the 60% to 100% range. So they need to complete at most 40% of their paintings.
Time needed: $1 h × 40\% = 24$ min
Mr. Daniel should give 24 more minutes.

18. Let h be the height.
$h^2 × \sqrt{h^2} × h = 16$
$h^2 × h × h = 16$
$h^4 = 16$
$h = 2$
Length: $2^2 = 4$ width: $\sqrt{4} = 2$
Surface area:
$4 × 2 × 4 + 2 × 2 × 2 = 40$
Its surface area is 40 cm².

19. By consecutive interior angles:
$x + 76° = 180°$
$x = 104°$
By opposite angles: $a = 76°$
By angles in a triangle:
$b + 76° + 44° = 180°$
$b = 60°$
By consecutive interior angles:
$60° + y = 180°$
$y = 120°$
By angles around a point:
$104° + 120° + z = 360°$
$z = 136°$
$x:y:z = 104°:120°:136° = 13:15:17$
The ratio is 13:15:17.

20. Let f be the no. of fantasy novels.
$f + 2f + \frac{1}{6}(2f) = 20$
$f + 2f + \frac{1}{3}f = 20$
$3\frac{1}{3}f = 20$
$f = 6$
Percent: $6 ÷ 20 = 30\%$
30% of the novels are fantasy novels.

ISBN: 978-1-77149-205-8

Unit 6

1. Side length of square cut-out: $\sqrt{49} = 7$

   Length: 55.8–7–7 = 41.8

   Height: 7

   Width: 33.4–7–7 = 19.4

   Capacity of box:

   41.8 × 19.4 × 7 = 5676.44

   The capacity of the box is 5676.44 mL.

2. Let w be the amount of water.

   $(1 + w) \times 20\% = 1 \times 50\%$

   $0.2 + 0.2w = 0.5$

   $0.2w = 0.3$

   $w = 1.5$

   Donald should add 1.5 L of water.

3. Factors of 24: 1, 2, 3, 4, 6, 8, 12, 24

   Perfect squares: 4, 9

+	1	2	3	4	5	6
1	2	3	4	5	6	7
2	3	4	5	6	7	8
3	4	5	6	7	8	9
4	5	6	7	8	9	10
5	6	7	8	9	10	11
6	7	8	9	10	11	12

   ☐ Factors of 24

   ⊠ Perfect squares

   Probability: $\dfrac{14}{36} = \dfrac{7}{18}$

   The probability is $\dfrac{7}{18}$.

4. Let b be the base of the lawn.

   $b \times \dfrac{4}{3}b \div 2 = 384$

   $\dfrac{2}{3}b^2 = 384$

   $b^2 = 576$

   $b = 24$

   Area of parking lot: 24 × 24 = 576

   lawn:parking lot = 384:576 = 2:3

   The ratio is 2:3.

5. By consecutive interior angles:

   $a + b = 180°$

   $a + 3\dfrac{4}{9}a = 180°$

   $4\dfrac{4}{9}a = 180°$

   $a = 40\dfrac{1}{2}°$

   By corresponding angles:

   $c = a = 40\dfrac{1}{2}°$

   By angles in a triangle:

   $c + d + 90° = 180°$

   $40\dfrac{1}{2}° + d + 90° = 180°$

   $d = 49\dfrac{1}{2}°$

   The angles are $40\dfrac{1}{2}°$, $49\dfrac{1}{2}°$, and 90°.

6. Side length of land: $\sqrt{576} = 24$

   24 is a multiple of 8 but not 5.

   The posts should be 8 m apart.

7. Mean: (0.7 + (-1.2) + 1.3 + (-2.2) + (-3.4) + 1.3 + (-0.7)) ÷ 7 = -0.6

   Median: -3.4 -2.2 -1.2 (-0.7) 0.7 (1.3 1.3)

   median   mode

   The mean was -0.6°C, the median was -0.7°C, and the mode was 1.3°C.

8. butter:sugar = 1:2 = $\dfrac{1}{2}$

   Let s be the amount of sugar.

   $\dfrac{1}{2}s + s + 2.5s = 12 \times 12$

   $4s = 144$

   $s = 36$

   36 g of sugar is needed.

9. Let d be the discount in percent.

   $20.24 = (23 - 23d) \times (1 + 10\%)$

   $20.24 = (23 - 23d) \times 1.1$

   $18.4 = 23 - 23d$

   $23d = 4.6$

   $d = 0.2$

   The discount was 20%.

10. Elapsed time:

    6:15 p.m. – 3:25 p.m. = 2 h 50 min = $2\dfrac{5}{6}$ h

    Distance: $888 \times 2\dfrac{5}{6} + 156 \times 2\dfrac{5}{6} = 2958$

    They were 2958 km apart.

11. Units up: 40.5 ÷ 4.5 = 9

    Units to the left: 27 ÷ 4.5 = 6

    Marilyn is at (-2,5).

12.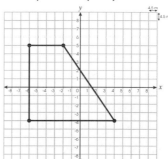

    Sum of bases of trapezoid:

    1275.75 × 2 ÷ 40.5 = 63

    Sum of bases in units: 63 ÷ 4.5 = 14

    Length of missing base: 14 – 4 = 10

    Move 10 units to the left from (4,-4) to reach the last corner at (-6,-4).

    The coordinates are (-6,-4).

13. Let c be the initial no. of chocolate bars.

    $c - 95 - \dfrac{2}{5} \times (c - 95) = 22\% \times c$

    $c - 95 - \dfrac{2}{5}c + 38 = 0.22c$

    $0.38c = 57$

    $c = 150$

    Corey started with 150 chocolate bars.

ISBN: 978-1-77149-205-8

14. By supplementary angles: $w + 116° = 180°$
$w = 64°$
By corresponding angles: $\angle CAB = w = 64°$
By supplementary angles: $\angle ABC + 80° = 180°$
$\angle ABC = 100°$
By angles in a triangle:
$\angle CAB + \angle ABC + \angle ACB = 180°$
$64° + 100° + \angle ACB = 180°$
$\angle ACB = 16°$

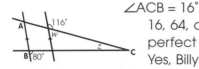

16, 64, and 100 are perfect squares.
Yes, Billy is correct.

15. GCF of 84 and 112: 28
No. of blue ribbons: $112 \div 28 = 4$
No. of red ribbons: $84 \div 28 = 3$
P(1 blue ribbon) $= \dfrac{4}{7}$
P(2 blue ribbons) $= \dfrac{4}{7} \times \dfrac{4}{7} = \dfrac{16}{49}$
The probability is $\dfrac{16}{49}$.

16. Chloe: $100 + 80 + 60 + (-20) + 30 + (-10) = 240$
Kimberly: $100 + 20 + (-40) + 70 + (-30) + 50 = 170$
Difference: $240 - 170 = 70$
The difference was $70.

17. Chloe's total: $240 + (-40) = 200$
Kimberly's total: $200 \times 40\% = 80$
Change: $80 - 170 = -90$
Kimberly's change of bank balance in June was -$90.

18. BC:CD:BD = $2:1:\overset{\times 3}{3} = 6:3:\underset{(2+1)}{9}$
Area of Section z: $6 \times 9 \div 2 = 27$
Area of square: $9 \times 9 = 81$
Area of Section y: $81 - 27 - 27 = 27$
The area of Section y is $27\ m^2$.

19. Let s be the number of $1.25 stamps.
$0.55 \times \dfrac{1}{2}s + 1 \times (28 - s - \dfrac{1}{2}s) + 1.25s = 28.2$
$0.275s + 28 - 1.5s + 1.25s = 28.2$
$0.025s = 0.2$
$s = 8$
Edward has 8 $1.25 stamps.

20.

Base (cm)					
	2	3	4	5	6
1	1	1.5	2	2.5	3
4	4	6	8	10	12
6	6	9	12	15	18
8	8	12	16	20	24

(Height (cm) labels the left column)

■: less than 10 cm²
Probability: $\dfrac{11}{20}$
The probability is $\dfrac{11}{20}$.

Unit 7

1.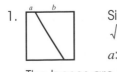

Side length of square:
$\sqrt{625} = 25$
$a:b:a+b = 1:4:\overset{\times 5}{5} = 5:20:\underset{(1+4)}{25}$
The bases are 5 cm and 20 cm long.

2. Let x be the number of times the watches rang at the same time.
LCM of 2 and 5: 10
Both watches rang at the same time every 10 min.
$\dfrac{10x}{2} + \dfrac{10x}{5} = 35$
$5x + 2x = 35$
$7x = 35$
$x = 5$
Time elapsed: $10 \times 5 = 50$
Time stopped:
8:00 a.m. + 50 min = 8:50 a.m.
Mary stopped the watches at 8:50 a.m.
The watches rang together 5 times.

3. Let c be the no. of cookies Mom baked.
$c - 32 - 32 - \dfrac{1}{4} \times (c - 32 - 32) = 15\% \times c$
$c - 64 - 0.25c + 16 = 0.15c$
$0.6c = 48$
$c = 80$
Mom baked 80 cookies.

4. P(winning blue raffle) $= \dfrac{1}{10}$
P(winning pink raffle) $= \dfrac{1}{8}$
P(winning both raffles) $= \dfrac{1}{10} \times \dfrac{1}{8} = \dfrac{1}{80}$
The probability is $\dfrac{1}{80}$.

5. By opposite angles: $w = 3.1x$
By angles in a triangle:
$1.7x + 3.1x + 1.2x = 180°$
$6x = 180°$
$x = 30°$
$w = 3.1x = 93°$
The measure of w is 93°.

6. Volume: $(6 + 8) \times 4.5 \div 2 \times 3.2 = 100.8$
Weight: $100.8 \times 0.95 = 95.76$
Cost: $0.05 \times 95.76 = 4.788$
Alice paid $4.79.

7. Try 6 and 8. ← $6^2 = 36$ and $8^2 = 64$

	6 and 8	36 and 64
GCF	2	4

4 is the square of 2 ($4 = 2^2$).
No, Boris is incorrect. The square of the GCF of the numbers (6 and 8) is the GCF of their squares (36 and 64).

8. Let f be the number of $5 bills.
$5f + 10 \times \dfrac{3}{2}f + 0.25 \times 2\dfrac{1}{2}f = 50 - 8.75$
$5f + 15f + 0.625f = 41.25$
$20.625f = 41.25$
$f = 2$
No. of $10 bills: $\dfrac{3}{2}f = 3$
No. of quarters: $2\dfrac{1}{2}f = 5$
Ezra got 2 $5 bills, 3 $10 bills, and 5 quarters.

ISBN: 978-1-77149-205-8

9. No. of students: $2 + 9 + 7 + 3 + 4 = 25$
Mean score: $(52 \times 2 + 74 \times 9 + 80 \times 7 + 84 \times 3 + 92 \times 4) \div 25 = 78$
Percent higher than mean:
$(7 + 3 + 4) \div 25 = 56\%$
56% of the students scored higher than the mean score.

10. Ken's box: $\overset{\div 2}{\overbrace{7:6}}:8 = 3.5:3:4$
Volume: $3.5 \times 3 \times 4 = 42$
Erin's box:
Length: $3.5 - 3.5 \times 20\% = 2.8$
Width: $3 - 3 \times 20\% = 2.4$
Height: $4 - 4 \times 20\% = 3.2$
Volume: $2.8 \times 2.4 \times 3.2 = 21.504$
Difference: $42 - 21.504 = 20.496$
The volume of Ken's box is 20.496 dm³ greater than Erin's.

11. Total path: 40 units
Quadrant I: $8 \div 40 = 20\%$
Quadrant II: $17 \div 40 = 42.5\%$
Quadrant III: $7 \div 40 = 17.5\%$
Quadrant IV: $8 \div 40 = 20\%$
65% of the path: $40 \times 65\% = 26$
20%, 42.5%, 17.5%, and 20% of Ally's path were in Quadrants I, II, III, and IV respectively. Ally's coordinates were (-6,4).

12. Time elapsed:
4:21 p.m – 3:17 p.m. = 1 h 4 min = 64 min
Distance: $0.2 \times 40 = 8$
Speed: $8 \div 64 = 0.125$ (km/min)
Distance in km: $0.125 \times 8 = 1$
Distance in units: $1 \div 0.2 = 5$
Ally would be at (-3,-2) after 8 min.

13. $(-3)^2 = 9$ $-2^2 = -4$ $(\sqrt{9})^2 = 9$
$\dfrac{5}{-6} = -\dfrac{5}{6}$ $(\sqrt{-1})^2 = -1$

×	+	+	–	–	–
+	+	+	–	–	–
+	+	+	–	–	–
–	–	–	+	+	+
–	–	–	+	+	+
–	–	–	+	+	+

Positive product:
$13 \div 25 = 52\%$
Negative product:
$12 \div 25 = 48\%$
Difference:
$52\% - 48\% = 4\%$

It is more likely to have a positive product by 4%.

14. $b \times 15 \div 2 \times 8 = \dfrac{3}{5} \times (24 + 24 - b) \times 15 \div 2 \times 8$
$60b = 36 \times (48 - b)$
$60b = 1728 - 36b$
$96b = 1728$
$b = 18$
b is 18 cm.

15. By angles in a triangle:
$(4x + 1) + (5x + 2) + (3x - 3) = 180°$
$12x = 180°$
$x = 15°$
$4x + 1 = 61°$
$5x + 2 = 77°$
$3x - 3 = 42°$
By alternate angles: $a = 42°$, $c = 61°$
By angles in a triangle:
$42° + b + 61° = 180°$
$b = 77°$
The measures are 42°, 77°, and 61° for a, b, and c respectively.

16. Total:
$3 + 5 + 4 + 9 + 6 + 13 = 40$
12.5% of total: $40 \times 12.5\% = 5$
The range 25 g to 30 g encompasses 12.5% of all seashells.

17. P(heavier than 25 g) $= \dfrac{5 + 3}{40} = \dfrac{8}{40} = \dfrac{1}{5}$
P(lighter than 20 g) $= \dfrac{4 + 9 + 6 + 13}{40}$
$= \dfrac{32}{40} = \dfrac{4}{5}$
Probability: $\dfrac{1}{5} \times \dfrac{4}{5} = \dfrac{4}{25}$
The probability is $\dfrac{4}{25}$.

18. Volume of house:
$(8.5 + 12.5) \times 6.4 \div 2 \times 5 + 12.5 \times 7.2 \times 5 = 786$
Total modelling clay: $786 \div 60\% = 1310$
Remaining modelling clay: $1310 - 786 = 524$
The volume is 524 cm³.

19. $6^2 + 8^2 + 9^2 = 36 + 64 + 82 = 181$
No, Rylan is incorrect. The sum of the angles in a triangle must be 180°.

20. Let r be the number of red marbles.
$r + 2r = 9$
$3r = 9$
$r = 3$
P(1 red marble) $= \dfrac{3}{9} = \dfrac{1}{3}$
P(3 red marbles) $= \dfrac{1}{3} \times \dfrac{1}{3} \times \dfrac{1}{3} = \dfrac{1}{27}$
The probability is $\dfrac{1}{27}$.

Unit 8

1. Let h be the number of hours.
$30 + 10.25(h - 2) = 28 + 8.75(h - 1)$
$30 + 10.25h - 20.5 = 28 + 8.75h - 8.75$
$1.5h = 9.75$
$h = 6.5$
Melody: $30 + 10.25 \times (7.8 - 2) = 89.45$
Amy: $28 + 8.75 \times (7.8 - 1) = 87.50$
They will charge the same amount at 6.5 hours. Lana should hire Amy.

ISBN: 978-1-77149-205-8

2. Volume of slice: $4\frac{1}{2} \times 8\frac{1}{3} \div 2 \times 6\frac{2}{5} = 120$
    Volume of middle section: $120 \div 3 = 40$
    The volume of the middle section is 40 cm³.

3. Mean:
    $((-4.64) + (-1.32) + 0.96 + 3.12) \div 4 = -0.47$
    Median: -4.64   -1.32   0.96   3.12
    $(-1.32 + 0.96) \div 2 = -0.18$
    The mean elevation is -0.47 m, the median elevation is -0.18 m, and there is no mode.

4. By consecutive interior angles:
    $126.8° + z = 180°$
    $z = 53.2°$
    By complementary angles:
    $53.2° + y = 90°$
    $y = 36.8°$
    By angles in a triangle:
    $x + 36.8° + 36.8° = 180°$
    $x = 106.4°$
    x is 106.4° and y is 36.8°.

    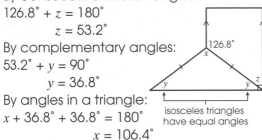
    isosceles triangles have equal angles

5. Mean amount in first two days:
    $30.2 \times 18\% = 5.436$
    Mean amount in next four days:
    $30.2 \times 12\% = 3.624$
    Amount collected in the first six days:
    $5.436 \times 2 + 3.624 \times 4 = 25.368$
    Amount collected on 7th day:
    $30.2 - 25.368 = 4.832$
    4.832 L of rainwater was collected.

6. LCM of 3, 5, and 7: 105
    Surface area: $105^2 \times 6 = 66\ 150$
    The surface area of the smallest cube is 66 150 cm².

7. Let p be the number of photos.
    $1 + 0.22p = 3.4 + 0.1p$
    $0.12p = 2.4$
    $p = 20$
    The prices will be the same for 20 photos.

8. By supplementary angles:
    $\angle ONM + 99° = 180°$
    $\angle ONM = 81°$
    By angles in a triangle:
    $\angle OMN + 76° + 81° = 180°$
    $\angle OMN = 23°$
    By supplementary angles:
    $\angle QOM + 76° = 180°$
    $\angle QOM = 104°$
    By isosceles triangle: $\angle OMQ = \angle MQO$
    By angles in a triangle:
    $104° + \angle OMQ + \angle MQO = 180°$
    $104° + 2\angle OMQ = 180°$
    $\angle OMQ = 38°$

    By angles in a triangle:
    $\angle QSM + 38° + 23° + 38° + 23° = 180°$
    $\angle QSM = 58°$

    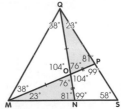

    There is a total of 8 triangles ($\triangle QMS$, $\triangle QMN$, $\triangle QNS$, $\triangle QMP$, $\triangle PMS$, $\triangle QMO$, $\triangle OMN$, $\triangle QOP$).
    There are 3 obtuse triangles ($\triangle QNS$, $\triangle PMS$, $\triangle QMO$).
    Obtuse triangles: $\frac{3}{8} = 37.5\%$
    37.5% of the triangles are obtuse triangles.

9. New rate: $11.5 + 11.5 \times 8\% = 12.42$
    Money earned before: $11.5 \times 27 = 310.5$
    Hours needed now: $310.5 \div 12.42 = 25$
    Difference: $27 - 25 = 2$
    Brendan works 2 fewer hours.

10. Side length before: $\sqrt{196} = 14$
    Side length after: $\sqrt{361} = 19$
    Thickness: $(19 - 14) \div 2 = 2.5$
    The thickness of the border is 2.5 cm.

11. Difference between grey and red:
    $28\% - 11\% = 17\%$
    Total no. of scarves: $85 \div 17\% = 500$
    Grey scarves: $500 \times 28\% = 140$
    Blue scarves: $500 \times 26\% = 130$
    White scarves: $500 \times 21\% = 105$
    Green scarves: $500 \times 14\% = 70$
    Red scarves: $500 \times 11\% = 55$
    There were 500 scarves in total. There were 140, 130, 105, 70, and 55 grey, blue, white, green, and red scarves respectively.

12. Let c be the cost of white and grey scarves.
    $(140 + 105)c + (130 + 70 + 55) \times (c + 2) = 6000$
    $245c + 255c + 510 = 6000$
    $500c = 5490$
    $c = 10.98$
    Cost of red, blue, green scarves: $c + 2 = 12.98$
    White and grey scarves cost $10.98 each and red, blue, and green scarves cost $12.98 each.

13. Old birdhouse: $5:7:9 = 20:28:36$ ⌐—×4—⌐
    New width: $20 + 20 \times 25\% = 25$
    New length: $28 + 28 \times 25\% = 35$
    New height: $36 + 36 \times 25\% = 45$
    New volume: $25 \times 35 \times 45 = 39\ 375$
    The volume is 39 375 cm³.

ISBN: 978-1-77149-205-8

14. Let c be the total no. of cookies.
$$c - c \times 67\% - \frac{1}{3}(c - c \times 67\%) = 66$$
$$c - 0.67c - 0.11c = 66$$
$$0.22c = 66$$
$$c = 300$$
Cookies sold: 300 − 66 = 234
Ms. Wood's class sold 234 cookies.

15. P(success of second test): $1 - \frac{1}{50} = \frac{49}{50}$

Bottles passed: $5000 \times 97\% \times \frac{49}{50} = 4753$

4753 bottles passed both tests.

16.
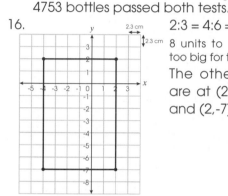

2:3 = 4:6 = 6:9 = 8:12
8 units to 12 units are too big for the grid.
The other corners are at (2,2), (-4,-7), and (2,-7).

17. Length: 2.3 × 9 = 20.7
Width: 2.3 × 6 = 13.8
Area: 20.7 × 13.8 = 285.66
Perimeter: (20.7 + 13.8) × 2 = 69
The area of the largest possible field is 285.66 m² and the perimeter is 69 m.

18. Oxygen used: 250 − 250 × 30% = 175
Time needed: 175 ÷ 1.4 = 125
It will take 125 minutes.

19. 6th test: 79% × 6 − 78% × 5 = 84%
7th test: 78% × 7 − 79% × 6 = 72%
Correct answers in 6th test: 50 × 84% = 42
Correct answers in 7th test: 50 × 72% = 36
Andre answered 42 and 36 questions correctly in the 6th and 7th tests respectively.

20. Triangle A: 60°, 60°, 60°
LCM of 60 and 60: 60
Triangle B: 45°, 36°, 99°
None of the angles is the LCM of the other two angles.
Triangle C: 80°, 80°, 20°
LCM of 20 and 80: 80
Saul could be describing Triangles A or C.

Unit 9

1. bananas to pears to total:
$3:7:10 \xrightarrow{\times 10} = 30:70:100$ (3+7)
Remaining bananas: $30 - 30 \times \frac{2}{5} = 18$
Remaining pears: 70 − 25 = 45

Ratio of bananas to pears: 18:45 = 2:5
The ratio of bananas to pears is 2:5 now.

2. Angle of ruler: 180° − 54° − 90° = 36° (supplementary angles)
Angle of teddy bear: 180° − 80° − 60° = 40° (supplementary angles)
P(ruler): $\frac{36°}{360°} = \frac{1}{10}$
P(teddy bear): $\frac{40°}{360°} = \frac{1}{9}$
P(ruler and teddy bear): $\frac{1}{10} \times \frac{1}{9} = \frac{1}{90}$
The probability is $\frac{1}{90}$.

3. 75 = 1 × 1 × 75
= 1 × 3 × 25
= 1 × 5 × 15
= 3 × 5 × 5

Possible dimensions	Surface area	
1 cm by 1 cm by 75 cm	302 cm²	✗
1 cm by 3 cm by 25 cm	206 cm²	✗
1 cm by 5 cm by 15 cm	190 cm²	✔
3 cm by 5 cm by 5 cm	110 cm²	✗

The dimensions are 1 cm by 5 cm by 15 cm.

4. Let t be the amount of tax.
$$30 - 30 \times 10\% + t + t = 32.4$$
$$27 + 2t = 32.4$$
$$2t = 5.4$$
$$t = 2.7$$
Discounted cost: $30 − $30 × 10% = $27
Tax rate: $2.70 ÷ $27 = 10%
The tax rate was 10%.

5. Volume of original prism:
12.8 × 12.8 ÷ 2 × 8.5 = 696.32
Volume of prism cut: 3.2 × 3.2 × 8.5 = 87.04
Percent cut: 87.04 ÷ 696.32 = 12.5%
Area to be painted:
(12.8 × 12.8 ÷ 2 − 3.2 × 3.2) × 2 + (12.8 − 3.2) × 8.5 × 2 + 3.2 × 8.5 × 2 = 360.96
12.5% of the original prism will be cut.
360.96 cm² needs to be painted.

6. For example, 12 and 18 are not perfect squares.
LCM of 12 and 18: 36 ← 36 is a perfect square.
Yes, 2 numbers that are not perfect squares can have an LCM that is a perfect square.

7. By opposite angles: $\angle ABC = \frac{380°}{3} = 126\frac{2}{3}°$

By alternate angles: $\angle ACB = \frac{239°}{8} = 29\frac{7}{8}°$
By angles in a triangle:
$$\angle BAC + 29\frac{7}{8}° + 126\frac{2}{3}° = 180°$$
$$\angle BAC = 23\frac{11}{24}°$$

The angles are $23\frac{11}{24}°$, $29\frac{7}{8}°$, and $126\frac{2}{3}°$.

ISBN: 978-1-77149-205-8

8. Let w be the number of weeks.
$40 + 11.5w = 96 + (-16.5w)$
$28w = 56$
$w = 2$
Mia and Marcus will have the same amount of savings after 2 weeks.

9. Let c be the weight of the original cake.
$(c - 12\% \times c) \times (1 - \frac{3}{4}) = 0.572$
$0.22c = 0.572$
$c = 2.6$
The weight of the original cake was 2.6 kg.

10. $(5.25 + 5.25 \times 300\%) \div 0.75 = 28$
Darla needs to sell 28 cups of lemonade.

11. Elevator usage in August: $70\% \times 8 - 90\% - 80\% - 85\% - 75\% - 60\% - 65\% - 55\% = 50\%$
Stairs usage in August: $1 - 50\% = 50\%$
The usage of stairs in August was 50%.

12. Probability of elevator usage in May: 60%
Probability of stair usage in May: 40%
Probability of 3 elevators and 1 stairs:
$60\% \times 60\% \times 60\% \times 40\% = 8.64\%$
The probability was 8.64%.

13.

	Quarters	Loonies
Leo	q	$12 - q$
Mona	$2q$	$12 - 2q$

Let q be the number of Leo's quarters.
$\frac{2}{3}(0.25q + 1 \times (12 - q)) = 0.25 \times 2q + 1 \times (12 - 2q)$
$\frac{2}{3}(12 - 0.75q) = 12 - 1.5q$
$8 - 0.5q = 12 - 1.5q$
$q = 4$
Leo's loonies: $12 - 4 = 8$
Total amount: $\$0.25 \times 4 + \$1 \times 8 = \$9$
Leo has $9.

14. 2 trapezoidal prisms make 1 rectangular prism.

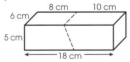

LCM of 5, 6, and 18: 90
Volume of 1 trapezoidal prism:
$(8 + 10) \times 5 \div 2 \times 6 = 270$
Volume of smallest cube-shaped box:
$90 \times 90 \times 90 = 729\ 000$
No. of trapezoidal prisms:
$729\ 000 \div 270 = 2700$
2700 trapezoidal prisms are needed. The box has a volume of 729 000 cm³.

15. $2^2 = 2 \times 2 = 4$ So, $\sqrt{4} = \sqrt{2^2} = 2$
$(-2)^2 = (-2) \times (-2) = 4$ So, $\sqrt{4} = \sqrt{(-2)^2} = -2$
Yes, Leon is correct. $\sqrt{4}$ is equal to both 2 and -2.

16. Point C: x-coordinate: $-4 \times \frac{1}{4} = -1$
y-coordinate: $4 \times \frac{1}{4} = 1$
Point D: $15 \div 2.5 = 6$ (units down)
Point E: $7.5 \div 2.5 = 3$ (units to the left)
Point F: x-coordinate: $-1 \times 2 = -2$
y-coordinate: $1 \times 2 = 2$

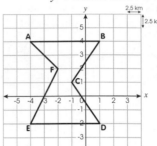

17. The area of Island ABCDEF is the difference between the area of Rectangle ABDE and the total area of Triangle AEF and Triangle BCD.
Area in square units:
$5 \times 6 - 6 \times 2 \div 2 - 6 \times 2 \div 2 = 18$
Area of 1 square unit: $2.5 \times 2.5 = 6.25$
Area in km²: $6.25 \times 18 = 112.5$
The area of the island is 112.5 km².

18. Let p be the probability of rolling an even number.
$p^2 = 16\%$
$p^2 = \sqrt{0.16}$
$p = 0.4$
No. of even numbers: $20 \times 0.4 = 8$
There are 8 even numbers on the dice.

19.

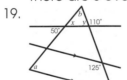

By opposite angles: $x = 50°$
By supplementary angles: $y + 110° = 180°$
$y = 70°$
By angles in a triangle: $b + 50° + 70° = 180°$
$b = 60°$
By consecutive interior angles:
$c + 125° = 180°$
$c = 55°$
By angles in a triangle: $a + 60° + 55° = 180°$
$a = 65°$
$a{:}b{:}c = 65°{:}60°{:}55° = 13{:}12{:}11$
The ratio is 13:12:11.

20. Height of stack:
$3013.2 \div 27.9 \div 21.6 = 5$ (cm) $= 50$ (mm)
No. of sheets: $50 \div \frac{1}{10} = 500$
There are 500 sheets of paper.

ISBN: 978-1-77149-205-8

Unit 10

1. Let t be the speed of the truck.

   $1.5t + 1.5 \times 1.2t = 214.5$

   $\qquad\qquad\quad 3.3t = 214.5$

   $\qquad\qquad\qquad\; t = 65$

   Speed of car: $65 \times 1.2 = 78$

   The average speed was 78 km/h for the car and 65 km/h for the truck.

2. $a = 9^2 = 81$

   $b = \sqrt{10\,000} = 100$

   By angles in a triangle:

   $b + x + x = 180°$

   $100° + 2x = 180°$

   $\qquad\quad x = 40°$

   By opposite angles: $c + x = a$

   $\qquad\qquad\qquad c + 40° = 81°$

   $\qquad\qquad\qquad\qquad c = 41°$

   c is 41°.

3.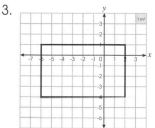

   Total possible area: $8 \times 5 = 40$

   Possible area in Quadrant III: $6 \times 4 = 24$

   Probability: $\dfrac{24}{40} = \dfrac{3}{5}$

   The total possible area is 40 m².

   The probability is $\dfrac{3}{5}$.

4.

Year	Rabbits	Foxes	Ratio
1	600	300	2:1
2	750	200	15:4
3	650	350	13:7
4	400	500	4:5
5	300	600	1:2
6	400	200	2:1
7	650	150	13:3

   There was a ratio of 2:1 in Years 1 and 6.

5.

Year	Rabbits	Foxes	Total	Percent of foxes
1	600	300	900	300 ÷ 900 = 33.33%
2	750	200	950	200 ÷ 950 = 21.05%
3	650	350	1000	350 ÷ 1000 = 35%
4	400	500	900	500 ÷ 900 = 55.56%
5	300	600	900	600 ÷ 900 = 66.67%
6	400	200	600	200 ÷ 600 = 33.33%
7	650	150	800	150 ÷ 800 = 18.75%

   35% of all animals were foxes in Year 3. The ratio was 13:7 that year.

6. Let b be the number of bills.

   No. of $10 bills: $0.4b$

   No. of $5 and $20 bills: $b - 0.4b = 0.6b$

   No. of $5 bills: $0.6b \div 2 = 0.3b$

   No. of $20 bills: $0.3b$

   $5 \times 0.3b + 10 \times 0.4b + 20 \times 0.3b = 345$

   $\qquad\qquad\qquad\qquad\qquad 11.5b = 345$

   $\qquad\qquad\qquad\qquad\qquad\quad\; b = 30$

   Melissa has 30 bills.

7. $\angle MNO = 59° + 31° = 90°$

   Shape MNO is a right triangle.

   Lines NO and MN are the base and height of $\triangle$MNO.

   By angles in a triangle:

   $\angle NOM + 33° + 59° + 31° = 180°$

   $\qquad\qquad\qquad\quad \angle NOM = 57°$

   Lines MO and RP are parallel by corresponding angles.

   Shape MOPR is a trapezoid.

   Area of Shape MNPR:

   $1.9 \times 3.3 \div 2 + (3.8 + 2.3 + 2.4) \times 2.5 \div 2 = 13.76$

   The area is 13.76 m².

8. LCM of 15 and 18: 90

   No. of sheets of star stickers: $90 \div 15 = 6$

   No. of sheets of heart stickers: $90 \div 18 = 5$

   Total cost: $3.20 \times 6 + $4.80 \times 5 = 43.20

   Total stickers: $90 + 90 = 180$

   Mean cost: $43.20 \div 180 = 0.24

   The mean cost of each sticker is $0.24.

9. GCF of 144, 160, and 208: 16

   $144 \div 16 = 9$

   $160 \div 16 = 10$

   $208 \div 16 = 13$

   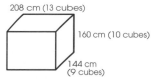

   The outer layer of each side is taken out to find the number of unpainted cubes.

   Unpainted cubes:

   $(9 - 2) \times (10 - 2) \times (13 - 2) = 7 \times 8 \times 11 = 616$

   616 cubes are unpainted.

10. There are 8 possible outcomes.

    Add: $1\frac{3}{4} + (-\frac{3}{4}) = 1 \;\leftarrow\; a + b = b + a$

    Subtract: $1\frac{3}{4} - (-\frac{3}{4}) = 2\frac{1}{2}$ or $(-\frac{3}{4}) - 1\frac{3}{4} = -2\frac{1}{2}$

    Multiply: $1\frac{3}{4} \times (-\frac{3}{4}) = -1\frac{5}{16} \;\leftarrow\; a \times b = b \times a$

    Divide: $1\frac{3}{4} \div (-\frac{3}{4}) = -2\frac{1}{3}$ or $(-\frac{3}{4}) \div 1\frac{3}{4} = -\frac{3}{7}$

    The probability is $\dfrac{5}{8}$.

11. Let n be the number.

    $4n = 8^2 \div 2$

    $4n = 32$

    $\;\; n = 8$

    The number is 8.

ISBN: 978-1-77149-205-8

12. Factors of 30: 1, 2, 3, 5, 6, 10, 15, 30

Possible dimensions (m)	Perimeter (m)
1 by 30	$(1 + 30) \times 2 = 62$
2 by 15	$(2 + 15) \times 2 = 34$
3 by 10	$(3 + 10) \times 2 = 26$ ←
5 by 6	$(5 + 6) \times 2 = 22$ ←

less than 30

Probability: $\frac{2}{4} = \frac{1}{2}$

The probability is $\frac{1}{2}$.

13. Let s be Jackie's speed on local roads.

$84 \times \frac{54}{60} + s \times \frac{36}{60} = 96$

$75.6 + 0.6s = 96$

$0.6s = 20.4$

$s = 34$

Jackie's speed on local roads was 34 km/h.

14. Lucy's mom's soup: $4\frac{2}{5} \times 10\% = 0.44$

Lucy's soup: $4\frac{2}{5} - 0.44 = 3.96$

Difference: $3.96 - 0.44 = 3.52$

Lucy has 3.52 L more soup than her mom.

15.

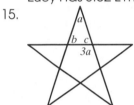

$3a = 540° \div 5$

$3a = 108°$

$a = 36°$

By supplementary angles:

$c + 3a = 180°$

$c + 108° = 180°$

$c = 72°$

By angles in a triangle:

$a + b + c = 180°$

$b + 36° + 72° = 180°$

$b = 72°$

b is 72°.

16. Side length: $\sqrt{64} = 8$

Total length of fencing: $8 \times 3 = 24$

Cost: $64.5 \times 24 = 1548$

Kyle needs to pay $1548 for fencing.

17. Before tax: $10.92 \div (1 + 12\%) = \$9.75$

Cost of 1 pizza: $\$9.75 \div \frac{3}{8} = \$26$

The price was $26.

18. Avery's mean score:

$(3 + (-1) + (-2) + 4 + (-5)) \div 5 = -0.2$

Benny's mean score:

$(-0.2) - 0.6 = -0.8$

Benny's score in Round 5:

$(-0.8) \times 5 - (-1) - 2 - (-4) - 6 = -7$

Benny's median score: -7 -4 ⊝1 2 6

Benny's median score was -1.

19.

Divide into 2 triangles:

Upper triangle: $(0.7 \times 6) \times (0.7 \times 2) \div 2 = 2.94$

Lower triangle: $(0.7 \times 6) \times (0.7 \times 4) \div 2 = 5.88$

Tota area: $2.94 + 5.88 = 8.82$

The area of the tub is 8.82 m².

20. Area in Quadrant IV:

$(0.7 \times 4) \times (0.7 \times 4) \div 2 = 3.92$

Area outside Quadrant IV: $8.82 - 3.92 = 4.9$

P(not in Quadrant IV) $= \frac{4.9}{8.82} = \frac{490}{882} = \frac{5}{9}$

P(2 people not in Quadrant IV)

$= \frac{5}{9} \times \frac{5}{9} = \frac{25}{81}$

3.92 m² of the tub is in Quadrant IV.

The probability is $\frac{25}{81}$.

ISBN: 978-1-77149-205-8